To My Grandson, Maxwell Jay

Timeline and Table of Contents

Introduction

From its top, Anthony's Nose, a mountain located along the Hudson River in New York State, offers a -180 degree, panoramic, awe-inspiring view of the Hudson Valley. It stands as the southern gateway to the Hudson Highlands, a series of 17 mountains on the east side of the Hudson River and 16 on the west side. Many historical and cultural events took place near Anthony's Nose. This book provides a bird's-eye view of 40 of these that had an impact on the area, the country and, in some cases, the world. Each has a story behind it, grounded in the historical (primary source) documents used here to tell. (Note: In this text, many quotations and excerpts from letters and other original texts use the original spelling and punctuation.)

The Bear Mountain Bridge spans the Hudson River in a view from the top of Anthony's Nose. photo by Christopher Cring

The name "Anthony's Nose" appeared on the original Dutch maps of 1697. Its origin remains uncertain: Washington Irving said the name was a trumpeter of New Amsterdam, some documents say an early ship captain inspired the name after pointing out a ledge (nose) that has since fallen off.

Old tourist postcards show Anthony's Nose.

During the Revolutionary War, Gen. William Alexander, a British aristocrat known as "Lord Stirling," who (despite his noble heritage) fought on the American side, sent a letter to George Washington. Dated June 1, 1776 it responded to Washington's request that Stirling analyze the area for defense against attacks by the British, based about 35 miles south in New York City. In his message, he mentioned

"A point of Land called Anthony's nose which is many hundred feet high, very steep & inaccessible, to any thing but Goats or men, very expert in Climbing; a Body of Riffle Men, placed here would be of very great use, in annoying an Enemy as the Decks of every Vessel that passes, must lie open to them."

Today Anthony's Nose, on the famous Appalachian trail (AT) is moderately accessible, so unless conditions have changed in a couple of hundred years, Lord Stirling was wrong: you don't have to be a goat or expert climber. The elevation is 900 feet, so on a clear day you can see 37 miles with a spyglass or binoculars.

Col. Rufus Putnam also analyzed Anthony's Nose for Washington and on Nov. 19, 1776, wrote a brief report:

Sir

"Sence your Exelency left this place I have Ben to Antonies Nose & I Beleve there is no danger of the Enimys attempting to possess it Nor will it Be Nesessary we Should occupye it".

But Anthony's Nose has seen much more than the Revolutionary War. From the mastodons who lived in the area to more modern visitors and residents, those who came participated in a wide range of activities. Many left stories. The author hopes that readers can relish them and relive past moments, organized here in chronological order and with the notion that it's nice to read a mixture of the whimsical and pure history.

1 The Tusked Giants: 10,000 years ago:

Related and similar to the modern elephant, mastodons roamed the Hudson Valley for many years before extinction. They could reach a height of 10 feet and weigh 10 tons. The Bear Mountain State Park museum has tusks and facial bones discovered in the area.

Life reconstruction of American Mastodon in 1897, by Charles knight courtesy of Wiki Commons. Simulated view of mastodons from Anthony's Nose by Christopher Cring

About 20 miles north, in Newburgh, Orange County, the world's first full skeleton of a mastodon was excavated, in 1799, on John Mastons farm. Charles Peale, a famous artist and Naturalist, bought the bones from Maston for $200 ($4200 today).

Deeply interested in the find, President Thomas Jefferson tried to buy the skeleton, too. At the time, Europeans, including Comte de Buffon, of France, ridiculed the new United States for not having any large animals in its history, The founders.archives.gov collection contains more than 20 Jefferson letters discussing this Newburgh discovery.

To excavate the mastodon, Charles Peale built a large wheel, which he brought up the Hudson River past Anthony's Nose on a barge. Peale then displayed the skeleton in his museum in Philadelphia. After Peale died, P. T. Barnum bought the museum, which later burned down. The mastodon escaped the fire and was purchased by Jakob Kaup for his museum in Hesse, Germany. A bomb air raid destroyed the museum in 1944 but the approximately 14,000-year-old mastodon skeleton was saved with little damage. In 2021, it was exhibited at the Smithsonian American Art Museum in Washington, D.C.

Exhuming the First American Mastodon, 1806 painting by Charles Willson Peale courtesy Wiki Commons

Over the years, many mastodons have been discovered in the Hudson Valley. One of the most recent discoveries was in Hyde Park, New York.

2 The Early Arrivals, 9500 years ago:

The first humans approached the Hudson Highlands in small groups along the river, across from Anthony's Nose. After the glaciers melted and the area became habitable, there were four different stages of growth leading up to Europeans' entry to the Highlands, and Henry Hudson's explorations.

The earliest inhabitants were the Palo-Americans, nomadic hunter-gatherers whose gear included primitive clovis-type projectile points and scrapers. They took shelter in mostly rock overhangs, and caves. They also made simple animal-hide dwellings. They preyed on large animals like the mastodon and beavers the size of today's bear. They also hunted small game, aquatic animals, fish, and gathered a variety of plants, nuts and berries. The small groups moved on frequently, leaving an area when its resources were depleted.

Bear Mountain State Park contains this basic rock shelter. Numerios tools and arrow points excavated in the area can be found in the Bear Mountain History Museum.

During the next period, the Archaic, about 5,000 years ago, semi-nomadic hunter-gatherers and fishers inhabited the land and engaged in no farming or pottery-making but extensively explored for nuts, seeds and shellfish. They utilized more advanced tools, including items of copper and built better dwellings than their predecessors; used soapstone for carved bowls and had cooking slabs.

The Transitional period, the third, occurred about 3,500 years ago. In it, the human residents, also semi-nomadic hunter-gatherers and fishers, crafted basic pottery, made more use of soapstone, and occupied the location longer. They also traded tools, food, and pelts with neighbors, had more advanced tools, and used hammer stones.

Installed on the patch of the Bear Mountain Zoo, this case displays arrow points and tools from a Native American Campsite along the Hudson River. Approximately 25 such sites have been identified along the river in Bear Mountain State Park.

About 3,000 years ago, in the Woodland period, when the societies grew more stable, populations increased and villages became common. Thanks to their farming, requirements to hunt and maintain a nomadic lifestyle decreased. There were also many advancements, such as improved stone and bone tools, the bow and arrow, leather-crafting, better boats, textile manufacturing, and shelter construction. Family trees also increased with culture. The first known recorded tribes native to this area during this period were the Lenape, Mohicans, Iroquois and the Algonquins.

In *Lost Arrowheads and Broken Pottery, about the history of Native Amaericans in Bear Mountain State Park, Edward J. Lenik details the results of many archaeological studies and provides information on trailside museums and displays.*

Bear Mountain museum offers an example of a Highlands-area village.

Peter Kalm, a Swedish explorer of the Hudson River Valley, was one of the only early explorers to document some of the early Native American culture in his 1747 journal, *Travels in North America.*

A few of Kalm's observations follow:

Clearing land for farming:

[The people strove] *to make good fields for maize-plantations; for if the ground where they intended to make a maize-field was covered with trees they cut off the bark all round the trees with their hatchets, that means the tree no more longer obstruct the rays of the sun. The smaller trees were then pulled out by main force, and the ground was a little turned up with crooked or sharp branches.*

Making canoes, some as long as 18 feet:

They set fire to a great quantity of wood at the roots of the tree, and made it fall by that means. But that the fire might not reach higher than they would have it, they fastened some rags to a pole, dipped them into water, and kept continually washing the tree, a little above the fire.

Whenever they intended to hollow cut a thick tree for a canoe, they laid dry branches all along the stem of the tree, as far as it must be hollowed out. They then put fire to those dry branches, and as soon as they were burnt, they were replaced by others. Whilst these branches were burning, the Indians were very busy with wet rags, and pouring water upon the tree, to prevent the fire from spreading too far on the sides and at the ends.

The tree being burnt hollow as far as they found it sufficient, or as far as it could without damaging the canoe, they took the above described stone-hatchets, sharp or flints, and quartzes, or sharp shells, and scraped off the burnt part of the wood, and smoothened the boats within By this means.

Tribes used fire to take down large trees at the base and fire and wet cloths to control the hollowing out the tree for a canoe.

Image courtesy Wiki Commons

Attire:

The women wear no head-dress, and have black hair. They have a short blue petti coat, which reaches to their knees, and the brim of which is bordered with red or other ribbands. They wear their shirts over their petticoats. They have large ear-rings and their hair is tied behind, and wrapped in ribbands. Their Wampum, or Pearls, and their money, which is made of shells, are tied round the neck, and hang down on the breast. This is their whole dress. They were now making several kinds of work of skins, to which they sowed the quills of the American Porcupines, having dyed them black or red, or left them in their original colour.

About eight o'clock three of the men arrived. Their hair was black, and cut short; they wore rough pieces of woollen cloth, of a bright green colour, on their shoulders, a shirt which covers their thighs, and pieces of cloth, or skins, which they wrap round the legs and part of the thighs. Two of them had painted the upper part of their foreheads, and their cheeks, with vermilion. Round their neck was a ribband, from which hung a bag down to the breast, containing their knives.

Rant-Che-Wai-Me, one of the few early images of early Americans from Indian Tribes of North America *by Thomas Mckenney and James Hall, 1837.*

Courtesy Library of Congress

Sept. 14-15, 1609, Henry Hudson: Henry Hudson sailed up the Hudson River, now named for him, exploring the area for a western passage to China. The Dutch West India Company funded Hudson and his ship the Halve Maen (Half Moon), which sailed north past Anthony's Nose and came up again on Oct. 1, on the return trip.

Henry Hudson courtesy Wiki Commons

Upon returning to the Netherlands, after exploring the River, Hudson reported that the inhabitants were open and willing to trade and barter and Hudson's crew could trade for furs and other items valuable to Europeans. Hudson also said the land was fertile for farming.

This report prompted the Dutch to soon fund many more trips and eventually colonize the area, which they called New Netherland. It included major fur-trading outposts along the Hudson River and the beginning of European settlements.

An image of the Half Moon on the Hudson River appears in Indian Tribes *Of Hudson's River 1700-1872, by Ruttenber, published 1872 courtesy Wiki Commons*

Robert Juet, Henry Hudson's master on board the Half Moon, wrote a journal about the 1609 trip. It is in the Library of Congress. Below are extracts of the Journal for the section of river south of Anthony's Nose, which they reached on Sept. 14-15, and from when they sailed past Anthony's Nose on the return trip, Oct 1.

Sunday, Sept. 6. *In the morning was fair weather, and our master sent John Colman, with four other men in our boat over to the north side, to sound the other river, being four leagues from us. They found by the way shoal water two fathoms; but at the north of the river eighteen, and twenty fathoms, and very good riding for ships; and a narrow river to the westward between two islands The land they told us were as pleasant with grass and flowers, and goodly trees, as ever they had seen, and very sweet smells came from them. So they went in two leagues and saw an open sea, and returned; and as they came back, they were set upon by two canoes, the one having twelve, the other fourteen men. The night came on, and it began to rain, so that their match went out; and they had one man slain in the fight, which was an Englishman, named John Colman, with an arrow shot into his throat, and two more hurt. It grew so dark that they could not find the ship that night, but labored to and fro on their oars. They had so great a stream that their grapnel would not hold them.*

Sept. 7. *Was fair, and by ten o'clock they returned aboard the ship, and brought our dead man with them, whom we carried on land and buried, and named the point after his name, Colman's Point. Then we hoisted in our boat, and raised her side with waste boards for defence of our men. So we rode still all night, having good regard to our watch.*

Sept. 8. *Was very fair weather, we rode still very quietly. The people came aboard us, and brought tobacco and Indian wheat, to exchange for knives and beads, and offered us no violence. So we fitting up our boat did mark them, to see if they would make any show of the death of our man; which they did not.*

Sept. 9. *Fair weather. In the morning, two great canoes came aboard full of men; the one with their bows and arrows, and the other in show of buying of knives to betray us; but we perceived their intent. We took two of them to have kept them, and put red coats on them, and would not suffer the other to come near us. So they went on land, and two others came aboard in a canoe; we took the one and let the other go; but he which we had taken, got up and leaped over-board. Then we weighed and went off into the channel of the river, and anchored there all night.*

Sept. 11. *Was fair and very hot weather. At one o'clock in the afternoon, we weighed and went into the river, the wind at south-south-west, little wind. Our soundings were seven, six, five, six, seven, eight, nine, ten, twelve, thirteen, and four teen fathoms. Then it shoaled again, and came to five fathoms. Then we anchored and saw that it was a very good harbour for all winds, and rode all night. The people of the country came aboard of us, making show of love, and gave us tobacco and Indian wheat, and departed for that night; but we durst not trust them.*

Sept. 12. *Very fair and hot. In the afternoon at two o'clock we weighed, the wind being variable, between the north and the north-west; so we turned into the river two leagues and anchored. This morning at our first rode in the river, there came eight and twenty canoes full of men, women and children to betray us; but we saw their intent, and suffered none of them to come aboard us. At twelve o'clock they departed. They brought with them oysters and beans, whereof we bought some. They have great tobacco pipes of yellow copper, and pots of earth to dress their meat in. It floweth south-east by south within.*

Sunday, Sept. 13. *Fair weather ; the wind northerly; at seven o'clock in the morning, as the flood came we weighed, and turned four miles into the river; the tide being done we anchored. Then there came four canoes aboard, but we suffered none of them to come into our ship; they brought very great store of very good oysters aboard, which we bought for trifles.*

In the night I set the variation of the compass, and found to be 130- In the afternoon we weighed and turned in with the flood two leagues and a half further and anchored all night, and had five fathoms soft oozy ground, and had a high point of land, which shewed out to us, bearing north by east five leagues off us.

Sept. 14. *In the morning being very fair weather, the wind south-east, we sailed up the river twelve leagues, and had five fathoms and five fathoms and a quarter less, and came to a strait between two points, and had eight, nine and ten fathoms; and it trended north-east by north one league, and we had twelve, thirteen and fourteen fathoms; the river is a mile broad; there is very high land on both sides. Then we went up north-west, a league and a half deep water; then north-east by north five miles; then north-west by north two leagues and anchored. The land grew very high and mountainous ;the river is full of fish.*

Sept. 15. *The morning was misty until the sun arose, then it cleared; so we weighed with the wind at south, and ran up into the river twenty leagues, passing by high mountains. We had a very good depth, as six, seven, eight, nine, ten, twelve, and thirteen fathoms, and great store of salmon in the river. This morning our two savages got out of a port and swam away. After we were under sail they called to us in scorn. At night we came to other mountains, which lie from the river's side; there we found very loving people, and very old men, where we were well used. Our boat went to fish, and caught great store of very good fish.*

The return trip after sailing north to Kinderhook and passing by Anthony's Nose:

Thursday, Oct. 1. *The first of October, fair weather, the wind variable between west and the north. In the morning we weighed at seven o'clock with the ebb, and got down below the mountains, which was seven leagues; then it fell calm and the flood was come, and we anchored at twelve o'clock. The people of the mountains came aboard us, wondering at our ship and weapons. We bought some small skin of them for trifles.*

This afternoon one canoe kept hanging under our stem with one man in it, which we could not keep from thence, who got up by our rudder to the cabin window, and stole out my pillow, and two shirts, and two bandelettes. Our master's mate shot at him, and struck him on the breast, and killed him. Whereupon all the rest fled away, some in their canoes, and so leaped out of them into the water. We manned our boat and got our things again. Then one of them that swam got hold of our boat, thinking to overthrow it; but our cook took a sword and cut off one of his hands, and he was drowned. By this time the ebb was come, and we weighed and got down two leagues—by that time it was dark; so we anchored in four fathoms water, and rode well.

Landing of Henry Hudson, 1609, at Verplanck Point (south of Anthony's Nose) Robert Weir, (Hudson River School) 1835; courtesy Wiki Commons

April 1762, Doodletown: Doodletown, New York, was an early Dutch, colonial, small town of approximately 70 families that is now a "ghost" (abandoned) town. The Dutch word "doodle" means "dead valley."

Doodletown is directly across from Anthony's Nose.

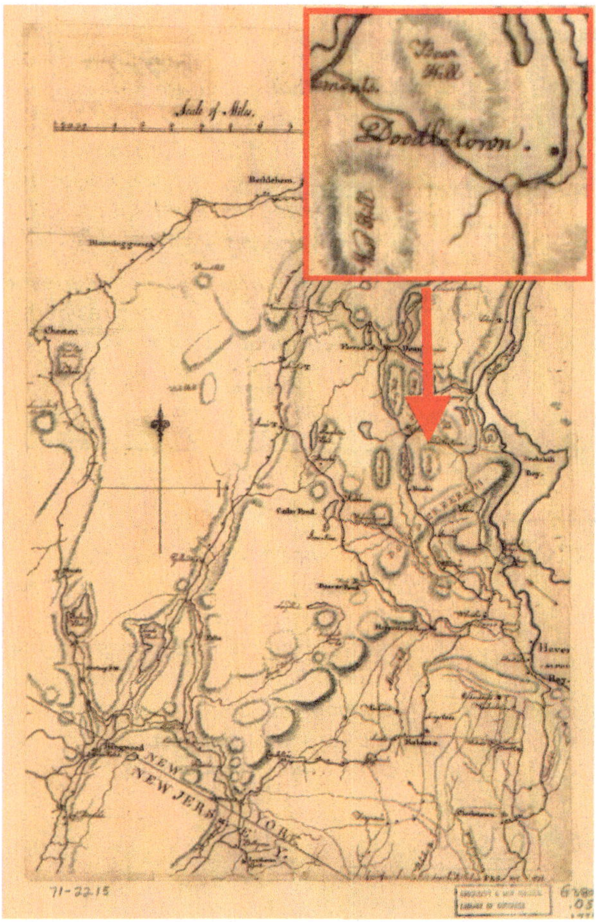

A map created in 1779 by Nathanael Greene (future Revolutionary War general) clearly shows Doodletown at the base of mountains. Image courtesy of the Library of Congress

Doodletown and the land in the area were purchased by the Cortlandt family from Indigenous occupants including the Lenape People. Soon after, the June family purchased 72 acres and became the first Doodletown settlers. The town grew quickly after iron mines in the area needed workers.

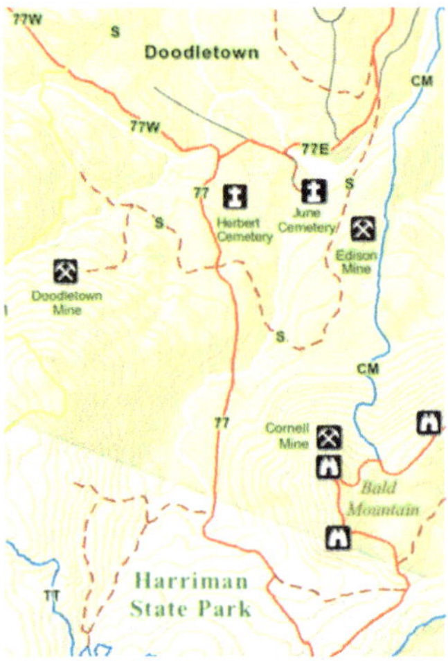

A Bear Mountain State Park map shows the three iron mines; Doodletown Mines, Cornel Mine and the Edison Mine. Thomas Edison used this mine to test new mining technology.

The June and Herbert Cemeteries are still used today by former residents and their families.

Maps provided by Bear Mountain Park give visitors a good layout of the town, since only foundations, steps and walkways remain. The tour is a 3-mile walk. Doodletown, like communities throughout the country, whose mines closed for various reasons, eventually became empty and derelict.

State park signs, a cemetery and steps await visitors along the walking tour.

During the Revolutionary War the people of Doodletown were startled on Oct. 6, 1777, when British Gen. Henry Clinton landed his ships close by, at Stony Point, and 2,100 Redcoats came on shore. They marched through Doodletown on their way around the mountain to attack and capture Fort Montgomery. The sight of 2,100 soldiers with carts, horses, and wagons marching through Doodletown was frightening to the residents. Also, when the battle started, the noise of the cannons firing from the fort, and the many British ships returning fire, was extremely loud.

A New York State marker indicates the march through Doodletown.

Oct. 6, 1777, The Battles of Forts Clinton and Montgomery:

Both American Revolutionary Forts were located on the Hudson River across from Anthony's Nose. The British, who occupied New York City, sailed up the Hudson River under the cover of an early morning fog, and attacked and captured both.

With the help of Loyalists Beverly Robinson and his son, who both knew the mountains from hunting, they surprised the Americans and attacked from the back of the forts. In the years before the war, Beverly Robinson had married Susanna Philipse, heiress to the British government patent for the Highland land that included Philipstown. When the war broke out, Robinson sided with the British. The Continental Army seized his house and Gen. Benedict Arnold, then fighting on the American side, took over the house as his headquarters. After capturing Forts Montgomery and Clinton, the British sailed up the Hudson River; cleared any American defenses, including the first chain across the river; and proceeded north to the hamlet of Kingston, which they burnt. The Fort Montgomery site is now a state historic park with a museum.

British and Hessian soldiers went through the mountains to attack Fort Montgomery. pictures courtesy Bear Mountain State Park.

The first American Hudson River-defense chain that the British destroyed stretched from Fort Montgomery to the base of Anthony's Nose. A few years later, revolutionary troops installed a new chain across the river from West Point to Constitution Island, just outside of the present village of Cold Spring (then a tiny hamlet of a few buildings). This chain remained until the end of the war.

The map below, from the British National Archives (with a copy available in the Library of Congress) clearly shows Anthony's Nose Its caption says:

"The plan of the attack of the Forts Clinton and Montgomery, upon Hudsons River, which were stormed by his Majesty's forces under the command of Sir Henry Clinton, K.B., on the 6th of Octr. 1777. " London, Wm Faden, 1784.

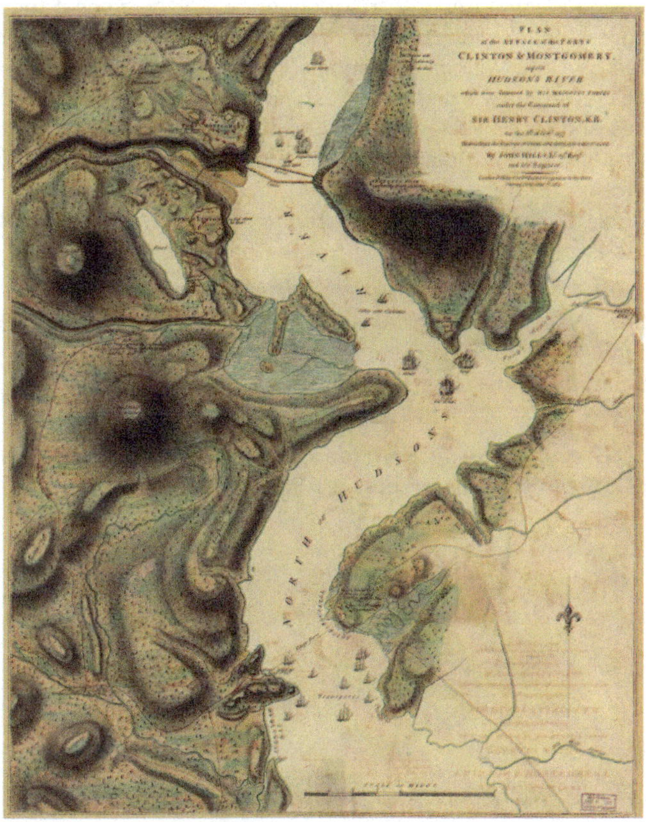

Oct. 30, 1777: George Washinton assigned 21-year-old-Alexander Hamilton to what the founders online government archive describes as one of the most delicate and important missions of his military career.

After victories in a couple of battles, including the one at Saratoga, Gen. Horatio Gates, a British-Born Continental Army officer recommended by Washington to the Continental Congress, proposed to replace Washington believing himself a better leader. Gates, who criticized Washington in correspondence, had had some members of congress on his side, plus a few officers. Washington learned of the revolt by Gen. William Alexander (Lord Stirling), who after seeing a Gates letter, forwarded it to Washington. Washington needed to stop Gates and let him know that he would not tolerate any of his officers discrediting him or disobeying his orders. This "near-coup" by Gates and other officers was called the "Conway Cabal", after Maj. Gen. Thomas Conway, who wrote letters criticizing Washington. Many of these letters were forwarded to the Continental Congress.

Gen. Washington sent Alexander Hamilton to see Gates, then in Albany, N.Y., and ensure he followed orders. An excerpt of Washington's message to Hamiltons follows:

To Alexander Hamilton from George Washington, 30 October 1777 From Headquarters, Philada

Dear Sir

It having been judged expedient by the Members of Council of War held yesterday, that one of the Gentlemen of my family should be sent to Genl: Gates in order to lay before him the State of this Army; and the Situation of the Enemy and to point out to him the many happy Consequences that will accrue from an immediate reinforcement being sent from the Nothern Army; I have thought it proper to appoint you that duty, and desire that you will immediately set out for Albany, at which place or in the neighbourhood, I imagine you will find Genl: Gates

George Washington, Alexander Hamilton and Horatio Gates, courtesy U.S. Parks Service and Wiki Commons

Washington assigned Capt. Caleb Gibbs, the first in command of his elite guard, to go with Hamilton on this mission. They started from Valley Forge on Oct 30, 1777 and returned to Washington on Jan. 20, traveling through the Hudson Valley to Albany and back. The mission was successful. Their actual expense account (from the founders archive), with the itinerary of the entire trip, verbatim, gives a glimpse of what travel was like in 1777; and includes details of food, lodging and transportation. It appears below:

Amount of expenses of Colo. Hamilton & Captain Gibbs. To Albany & back again – set off from Skippack road, 15 miles from Phila: Returned to Valley Forge –Sent by His Excelly. Genl. Washington on public service.

1777.

October	*30th.*	*Cash paid at Correls. Ferry Lodgg - Sup. horses*
	31	*at crossroads N.Jersey*
Novr	*1*	*at Chester.- 1.17.4 -2nd at N.Windsor ferry 8/6*
	4	*at Paukeepsey - 19/ – at Rhynbeck 25/6*
	5th	*at Clauverick – 16/8 – gave a guide– 9/*
		at Kinderhook – 16/ – at Albany ferry 6/
	8th	*at Cosockett– 19/6 -at Well's ferry – 5/*
		at Pools Landing 24/6 - 9th on the road to

Clauvierck 10

10th at Clauverick - 14/ at Tatias tavern dinner & c 12/

11th at the flats 18/6 - at paukeepsey 10/6

12th at Fish Kill- 30/ - at New Windsor ferry 10/

14th at Goshen- 20/- at Chester 27/

16th at Pompton- 14/

On the road to PeeksKill when Colo. Hamilton was taken sick from Morrris Town.

22d at Ramapaugh 13/ -at Cacaat (Kakiate) -16/8

23 at Kings ferry . - gave the ferryman 5/

Cash paid at Peeks Kill when Colo. Hamilton Was sick

25th to 3 quarters mutton @ 8/24 gave the doctor 6/

Decembr 4th to 12 fouls-for the whole5 dollars-

7 to Cash for Oranges & Shrub 15/ 10th to potatoes 10

12th to 3 dozen Eggs @ 5. To15/; 19th to potatoes 5/

21 to quails - 5/ - To a partridge 2/6

23d. To Mr. Kennedys Bill - 12.0-To Cash for a bed 45/

To washing &c.-- 15/

Expices to Head Quarters from Peeks Kill-

Decembr 23d at Kings ferry 8/- at Cacaar horse. Lodge Breakft &c

DEcembr 24th Cash paid at Ramapaugh dinig hotels &c

Decembr 25th at Pompton -37/6 at Hardoorits

1778

Januay- 5th Paid Coach for his Expences to Peeks Kill-

8 at Cross Roads New Jersey-

12th at White house tavern 47/6 at -

13th at Oakhams near Deleware-

15th at Latharams-

17-18-19th 20 To cash paid between Newton & Schuylkill-

A lot of the time was spent in Peekskill, when Hamilton was sick. Peekskill is just south of Anthony's Nose.

September 22, 1780: Benedict Arnold treason uncovered with help of Continental soldier "Rifle Jack" (John Peterson).

Benedict Arnold, 40 years old, was a successful major general in the Continental army before he decided to defect and become a British Loyalist. Highly respected by George Washington, he was now commander of West Point and the important Hudson River and surrounding Hudson Highlands. He planned to surrender West Point and the area to the British; he was also supplying the British with important strategic war-related intelligence. Had he succeeded, the effect would have been devastating.

On this day in September the following people were involved:

Benedict Arnold British Spy John Andre British Gen. Henry Clinton images courtesy Wiki Commons

John Andre, 23 years old, led British Gen. Sir Henry Clinton's espionage team. Educated in top schools, he knew four languages, was very talented in the arts, able to write, draw, paint, and sing. When the British occupied Philadelphia, he was living in the house where Benjamin Franklin had resided. During this time, Andre mingled with society, including Arnold's new wife, 20-year-old British Loyalist Margarat "Peggy" Shippen. Peggy was continually in contact with John Andre and helped with Arnold's secret negotiations with him.

Peggy Shippen *Alexander Hamilton* *George Washington*
images courtesy Wiki Commons

A Daughters of the American Revolution memorial honors "Rifle Jack" Peterson and Moses Sherwood. They were in the Westchester Militia and their firing at the British ship Vulture caused it to retreat downriver. British spy Andre then had to travel by horseback and was soon captured, exposing the plot.

John "Jack" Peterson, a soldier of African and Native American (Croton) descent, was considered a sharpshooter. He had a long career in the military, was also a prisoner of the British, and once escaped from a prison ship. He continued to live in the area long after the Revolutionary War, owned a house in Peekskill, had 11 children, and died at age 103.

HMS Vulture sailed up the Hudson to Westchester County. Andre came ashore in a rowboat on the west side of the Hudson with British soldiers, to have a secret meeting with Arnold, who was living at his headquarters at The Robinson House, across the Hudson from West Point. Peggy Shippen was at home as well, with their new child. The plan involved Arnold giving up West Point and an attempt to capture Washington. (see the full-page map and diagram of the area at the end of this section)

While Andre was on land with Arnold, shots fired by Peterson and Moses Sherwood could be heard from Anthony's Nose. Soon the musket shots turned into cannon shots fired from American Revolutionary soldiers on land and fire returned by the Vulture. This lasted two hours before the ship was forced to go further down the river, leaving Andre on shore.

After the meeting between Arnold and Andre ended, Arnold returned to the Robinson house. Since the Vulture was out of sight, Andre had to cross the river at Kings Ferry, about five miles south of Anthony's Nose, and ride back to New York City through Westchester. The next day he was captured by three American Revolutionary soldiers, who searched Andre, uncovered the plot and Arnold's treason, and found a pass from Arnold to Andre. Confusion ensued and the American's wrote a letter to Arnold explaining the capture.

Benedict Arnold quickly ordered a barge with his crew to row down the river to the Vulture and escape. Anyone on Anthony's Nose could see Arnold's barge go by. Washington soon arrived at the Robinson House with his entourage for a planned breakfast meeting and tour of West Point with Arnold. When Washington found Arnold was not there, he went with his aides across the river to inspect West Point. His trip across the water by barge could also be seen from Anthony's Nose. Washington found the fort in bad condition —Arnold had deliberately readied it to be taken over by the British—and suspected something was wrong. Washington returned across the river to the Robinson House and was greeted by Hamilton and Maj. Gen. Gilbert Lafette (the French marquis) with the papers found on Andre. They told Washington that Arnold had betrayed them.

Washington ordered Hamilton, James McHenry, and other dragoons (mounted soldiers) to quickly pursue Arnold. From Anthony's Nose, they could be seen riding along the river, trying to catch up with Arnold. They were too late; Arnold was safe on the Vulture. From the ship he wrote a letter, carried by a flag-boat to Hamilton on the shore, which requested that Washington send his wife and child back to her parents in Philadelphia or to Arnold in New York City. Washington sent her to Philadelphia and from there she soon traveled to reach Arnold in New York City.

The escape of Arnold on the British Sloop-of-war "vulture", by Howard Pyle, 1853-1911.

courtesy Boston Public Library

The Founders.archives.gov contains letters from those involved:

From Major General Benedict Arnold, on Board the Vulture, to Gen. George Washington on Sept. 25:

The Heart which is Concious of its Own rectitude, Cannot attempt to paliate a Step, which the World may Censure as wrong; I have ever acted from a Principle of Love to my Country, since the Commencement of the present unhappy Contest between Great Britian and the Colonies, the same principle of Love to my Country Actuates my present Conduct, however it may appear Inconsistent to the World: who very Seldom Judge right of any Mans Actions.

I have no favor to ask for myself, I have too often experienced the Ingratitude of my Country to Attempt it: But from the known humanity of your Excellence I am induced to ask your protection For Mrs Arnold from every Insult and Injury that the mistaken Vengence of my Country may expose Her to: It ought to fall only on me—She is as good, and as Inocent as an Angel, and is Incapable of doing Wrong. I beg She may be permitted to return to Her Friends in Philada or to come to me as She may choose; from your Excellencey I have no fears on Her Account, but She may Suffer from the mistaken fury of The Country.

I have to request that the Inclosed Letter may be delivered to Mrs Arnold, and She permitted to write to me.

I have also to Ask that my Cloths & Baggage which are of little Consequence may be Sent to me, If required their Value shall be paid in Money. I have the honor to be With great reguard & Esteem Your Excellencys Most Obedt Hbl. Servt

B. Arnold

Maj. Gen. William Heath later wrote in his memoirs:

"Gen. Arnold's panic was so great, when he found that the plot was discovered, that he called out for a horse, any horse that first came to hand, if it were a wagon-horse; upon the horse being brought, the General mounted, and, instead of passing to the landing by the usual path, he rode down a steep bank, where it seemed impossible for a horse with a rider to get down, without being unhorsed."

Maj. Gen. Lafayette's aide-de-camp James McHenry apparently copied the enclosed, undated letter from Arnold to his wife, Peggy. It reads:

"Thou lovelies[t] & thou best of women words are wanting to express my feelings and distress on your account who are incapable of doing wrong yet are exposed to suffer wrong. I have requested his excellency General Washington to take you under his protection, and permit you to go to your friends in Philada—or to come to me. I am at present incapable of giving advice. follow your own intentions. But do not forget that I shall be miserable until we meet. Adieu kiss my dear boy for me. God Almighty bless & protect you ... Write me one line if possible to ease my anxious heart" (from: James McHenry Papers).

Washington's aide-de-camp, Hamilton, wrote to his fiancé Elizabeth Schuyler on Sept. 25:

"In the midst of my letter, I was interrupted by a scene that shocked me more than any thing I have met with—the discovery of a treason of the deepest dye. The object was to sacrifice West Point. General Arnold had sold himself to André for this purpose. The latter came but in disguise and in returning to New York was detected. Arnold hearing of it immediately fled to the enemy.

I went in persuit of him but was much too late, and I could hardly regret the disappointment, when on my return, I saw an amiable woman frantic with distress for the loss of a husband she tenderly loved—a traitor to his country and to his fame, a disgrace to his connections. It was the most affecting scene I ever was witness to.

She for a considerable time intirely lost her senses. The General went up to see her and she upbraided him with being in a plot to murder her child; one moment she raved; another she melted into tears; sometimes she pressed her infant to her bosom and lamented its fate occasioned by the imprudence of its father in a manner that would have pierced insensibility itself. All the sweetness of beauty, all the loveliness of innocence, all the tenderness of a wife and all the fondness of a mother showed themselves in her appearance and conduct. We have every reason to believe she was intirely unacquainted with the plan, and that her first knowle[d]ge of it was when Arnold went to tell her he must banish himself from his Country and from her forever. She instantly fell into a convulsion and he left her in that situation.

Lafayette wrote to Anne-Cesar, chevalier de La Luzerne, French minister to the United States, from Beverly Robinson's house on Sept. 26.:

"When I left you yesterday morning, Monsieur le Chevalier, to come here to breakfast with General Arnold, we were far from imagining the event that I am going to relate to you. ...

"West Point has been betrayed, and by Arnold. The same man who had covered himself with glory in rendering conspicuous service to his country had lately formed an appalling pact with the enemy. Were it not for the chance that brought us here at a certain hour and the chance that, through a combination of mishaps, caused the adjutant general of the British army to fall into the hands of a few peasants outside all our posts, West Point and the North River would now perhaps be in the possession of the enemy.

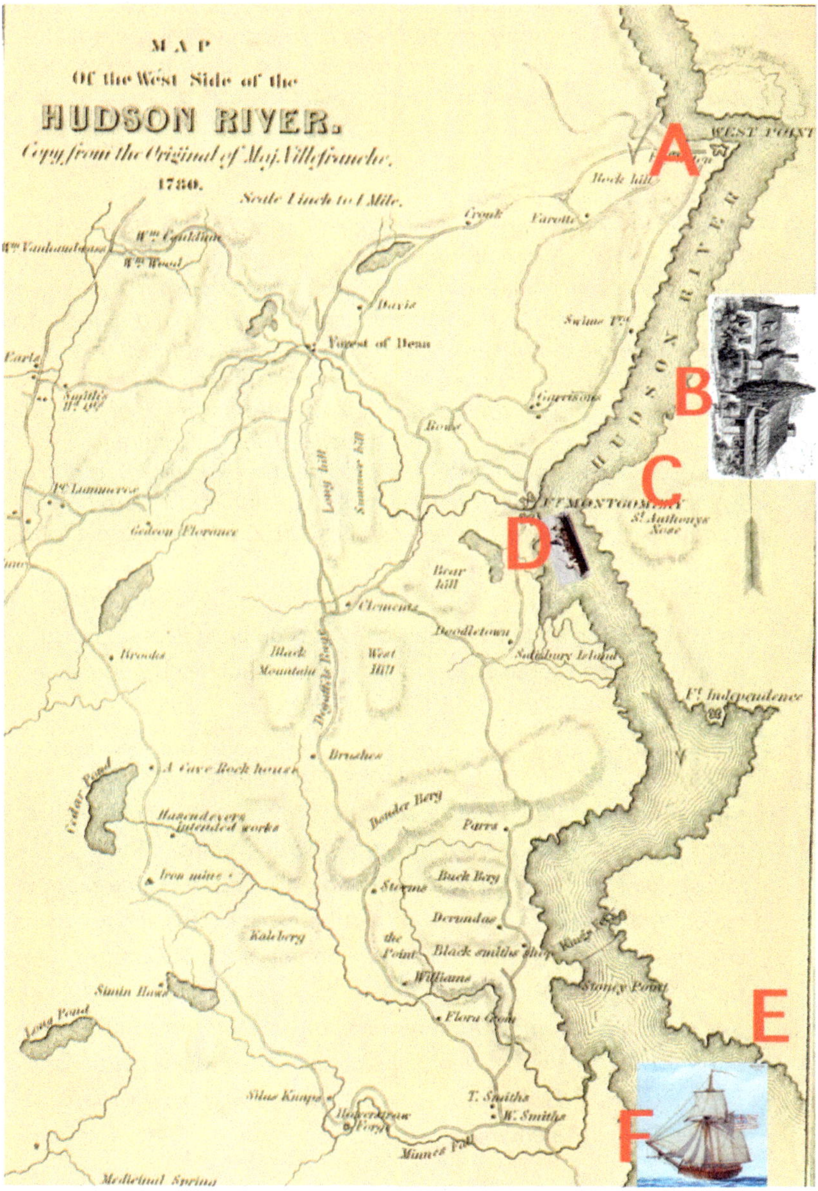
MAP
Of the West Side of the
HUDSON RIVER.
Copy from the Original of Maj. Villefranche.
1780.
Scale 1 inch to 1 Mile.
A
B
C
D
E
F
WEST POINT
Rock hill
HUDSON RIVER
Forest of Dean
Garrisons
Long hill
Summer hill
Ft MONTGOMERY
St Anthonys Nose
Bear hill
Clements
Black Mountain
West Hill
Salisbury Island
Ft Independence
Brushes
Donder Berg
Cedar Pond
Iron mine
Buck Berg
Parrs
Kakeberg
Black smiths shop
Williams
Stoney Point
Long Pond
T. Smiths
W. Smiths
Silas Knaps
Minnes Fall
Medicinal Spring

This map, from 1780 (Library of Congress), covers the area encompassed by the Benedict Arnold incident. Places listed include Anthony's Nose–which the cartography called St. Anthony's Nose.

A. West point included the fort Benedict Arnold intended to turn over to the British.

B. The Beverly Robinson house, where Benedict Arnold lived, was also his Highland headquarters. Robinson was a British Loyalist and the Continental had confiscated his house. Involved in the British spy ring, Robinson also fled on the British ship Vulture.

C. The top of Anthony's Nose mountain offers a bird's-eye, panoramic view.

D. Benedict Arnold's barge had his crew assigned to row, and with it he reached the Vulture and escaped.

E. From this approximate location, soldiers "Rifle Jack" (Jack Peterson), and Mosses Sherwood spotted the British ship and fired their muskets. Then they returned with a cannon and fired further at the Vulture, causing it to leave Andre on shore behind. Andre had to go by horseback to return to British-occupied New York. He was soon caught.

F. The British ship HMS Vulture was used to bring spy Andre to meet on the Western shore with Benedict Arnold to negotiate and get intelligence.

Aug. 20, 1781, Battle of Yorktown:

From Washington's Journal from Kings Ferry at Verplanck's Point on the Hudson River, a few miles south of Anthony's Nose:

"August 20th.-- The head of the Americans arrived at Kings Ferry about ten O'clock and immediately began to cross".

"August 21st–In the course of this day the whole of the American Troops, all their baggage, artillery & stores (supplies) crossed the river."

"August 22d, 23d, 24th, & 25th - Employed in transporting the French Army– its baggage and stores(supplies) over the river"

Gen. Washington, with about 3,500 troops and supplies, and French Gen. Jean-Bapriste Rochambeau, with 4,000 troops and supplies, were crossing the Hudson River on their way in a long exhausting journey to attack British Gen. Charles Cornwallis at Yorktown, Virginia. This would be the last major battle of the Revolutionary War and after seven years would be the one that would end the war.

During this crossing, Rochambeau told Washington he wanted to see West Point, since they were only nine miles away. So both traveled on a barge past Anthony's Nose and a few miles north to West Point.

Rochambeau by Charles Philippe Larivere and Washington by John Trumbull courtesy Wiki Commons

Before the journey to Yorktown started, the French army had marched from Providence, Rhode Island, and the Continental Army had marched from New Windsor, New York. The two armies would meet for the first time in Westchester County, New York, 12 miles from the crossing at Kings Bridge. Although very different, the two armies would soon forge a bond. Below are reviews of these first encounters from actual journals and diaries:

"August 22.- The troops arrived in a quite good season at their camp at King's Ferry, which was pitched on the brow of a hill overlooking the North River. (Hudson) They remained there on the 23d and 24th. During this time arrangements were made for the passage of the River by all the trains and troops,quite a difficult matter,there being but few boats. August 28.- As the Headquarters remained at Peskill [Peekskill], M. de Rochambeau, was not willing to pass so near West Point as nine miles,without seeing it. He left by boat at eight o'clock in the Morning to visit it with General Washington and several officers."— Diary of Baron Cromot du Bourg.

Sent ahead to White Plains on July 4 to report to Washington on the approach of the French army, Capt. Ludwig von Closen Haydenburg (known as Closen), Rochambeau's aide-de-camp, was the first of the French officers to see the Continental Army soldiers. Some of his observations (from Washington papers.org) follow:

"I had a chance to see the American army, man for man, It was really painful to see these brave men, almost naked, with only some trousers and little linen jackets, most of them without stockings, but would you believe it? very cheerful and healthy in appearance. A quarter of them were negroes, merry,confident, and sturdy." *image of Closen's biography*

Closen also wrote his impression of the American troops during a dress uniform parade for troop inspection.

"The whole effect was rather good. Their arms were in good condition; some regiments had white cotton uniforms. Their clothing consisted of a coat, jacket, vest, and trousers of white cloth, buttoned from the bottom to the calves, like gaiters. Several battalions wore little black caps, with white plumes. Only General Washington's mounted guard and Sheldon's legion wore large caps with bearskin fastenings as crests. Three-quarters of the Rhode Island regiment consists of negroes, and that regiment is the most neatly dressed, the best under arms, and the most precise in its maneuvers. The American army is always drawn up in two lines, a custom which we have also adopted."

This watercolor from the American War of Independence is by Jean Baptiste Antoine de Verger (1762-1851), a French artist who himself fought in the war in Yorktown as a sub-lieutenant in a French regiment and who kept an illustrated journal of his experiences in the war. The watercolor, which appears in the journal, shows the variety of soldiers fighting for American independence, depicting, from left to right, a black soldier of the First Rhode Island Regiment, a New England militiaman, a frontier rifleman, and a French officer. image courtesy of the library of Congress

The diary of a French officer, Baron Cromot du Bourg Marie Francois Joseph Maxime.

At Phillipsburg : " July 8.- In the afternoon of the 8th General Washington reviewed the two armies; we went first to the American army, which may have amounted to four thousand and some hundred men at the most. It seemed to me to be in as good order as possible for an army composed of men without uniforms and with narrow resources. The Rhode Island regiment, among others,is extremely fine. We then went there to the French army,which, though unpretending,has quite another style. The Americans admit it; they all seemed to be delighted as well as their General."

Another French officer, Lieut. Jean-Francois-Louis, comte de Clermont-Crevecoeur, also recorded thoughts about the American army.

"I went to the American camp, which contained approximately 4,000 men. In beholding this army I was struck, not by its smart appearance, but by its destitution: the men were without uniforms and covered with rags; most of them were barefoot. They were of all sizes, down to children who could not have been over fourteen. There were many negroes, mulattoes, etc. Only their artillerymen were wearing uniforms. These are the élite of the country and are actually very good troops, well schooled in their profession."

Map of Yorktown routes from the National Park Service.

Later in the march they exchanged some encounters with British soldiers and Closen (Washingtonpapers.org) commented:

"I admire the American troops tremendously! It is incredible that soldiers composed of men of every age, even of children of fifteen, of whites and blacks, almost naked, unpaid, and rather poorly fed, can march so well and withstand fire so steadfastly. The calm and calculated measures of General Washington, in whom I discover daily some new and eminent qualities, are already well known, and the entire universe accords him the homage of its highest esteem. He is certainly admirable as a leader of his army, in which everyone regards him as his friend and father."

The troops traveled 680 miles in 14 weeks. Since it was summer and hot they marched from 4 AM until 12 noon almost every day. On September 22 the two armies met the troops commanded by Marquis de Lafeyette and prepared for the battle of Yorktown. On September 28 after an extremely tiring and demanding march the troops began digging trenches that allowed the American and French to attack the British forces until they surrendered. The first trench was 800 yards from the British troops and was 2000 yards long. The second trench was 400 yards from the British line. The trenches were dug at night and split between the French and American troops.

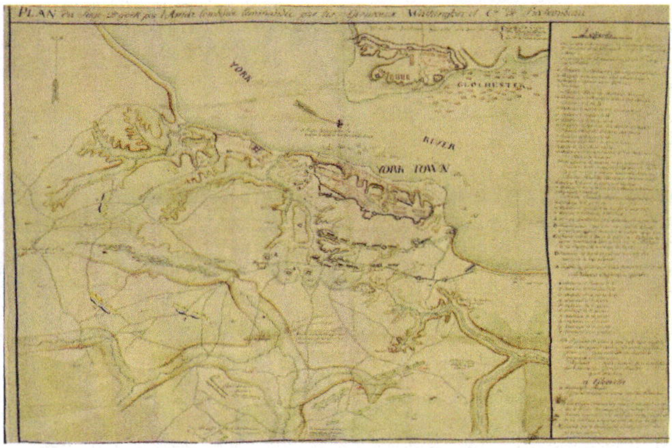

Battle of Yorktown strategy maps showing the trenches. courtesy Library of congress.

"Washington firing first shot" and "Storming redoubt number 10 lead by Alexander Hamilton," by Eugine Lami, courtesy Wiki Commons.

"Battle of Yorktown," by Auguste Colder and "Surrender at Yorktown," by John Trumble courtesy Wiki Commons.

Nov. 18, 1783, Emancipation of New York City:

George Washington left the West Point-Anthony's Nose area, to start his one-week journey to triumphantly march into New York City to celebrate liberty following seven years of British occupation. After the last major battle at Yorktown, followed by the Paris Peace Treaty, there were long negotiations and disagreements over the evacuation. British Gen. Sir Guy Carleton and Wasington, along with their staffs, sent many notes to each other and also met on May 5 in person, to work out all the details. Now was the time to celebrate the start of a new and free America and replace the British flags with the stars and stripes.

Gen. Henry Knox marched the remaining 800 Continental Army troops from Newburgh, and on Nov. 21, they crossed the Kings Bridge to Harlem Plain where they camped to be ready to march into New York City. Washington and George Clinton, governor of New York, and their aides met at the Blue Bell Tavern to prepare for the grand entrance.

Blue Bell Tavern, as depicted in The Itinerary of Gen. Washington

Below are the orders for the ceremony entering New York City, taken from *The Itinerary of General Washington (which apparently relied in part on a contemporary handbill):*

[See note below.]

" New York, Nov. 24,1783. The Committee appointed to conduct the Order of receiving their Excellencies Governor Clinton and General Wasgington, beg Leave to inform Fellow-Citizens, that the Troops,

under the command of Major-General Knox,will take Possession of City at the Hour agreed on, Tuesday next; as soon as this may be performed, he will request the Citizens who may be assembled on Horseback, at the Bowling-Green, the lower End of the Broad-Way, to accompany him to meet their Excellencies Governor Clinton and General Washington, at the Bull's Head, in the Bowery - the Citizens on Foot to assemble at or near the sea water Pump.

ORDER OF PROCESSION. A Party of Horse will precede their Excellencies and be on their flanks after the General and Governor, will follow the Lieutenant-Governor and Members of the Council for the temporary Government of the Southern Parts of the State- The Gentlemen on Horse-back, eight in Front- those on Foot, in the Rear of the Horse, in like Manner. Their Excellencies, after passing down Queen-Street, and the Line of Troops up the Broad-way, will a-light at Cape's Tavern. The Committee hope to see their Fellow Citizens, conduct themselves with Decency and Decorum on this joyful Occasion."- Contemporary hand-bill.

"George Wasgington's triumphal entry into New York City, Nov 25, 1783," by E.P. Restein and L.Restein, 1879 (left) and "Washington's Grand Entry into New York Nov 25th" 1783" by Alphonse Bigot; courtesy Wiki Commons.

After a week of speeches, band-playing, fireworks and the transition of the recapture of the city, it was time for George Washington to leave. On Dec. 4, at Fraunces Tavern, he had an emotional farewell dinner and said goodbye and thanked his staff, friends, and officers before leaving for the Continental Congress to relinquish his general commission and return to his home in Virginia.

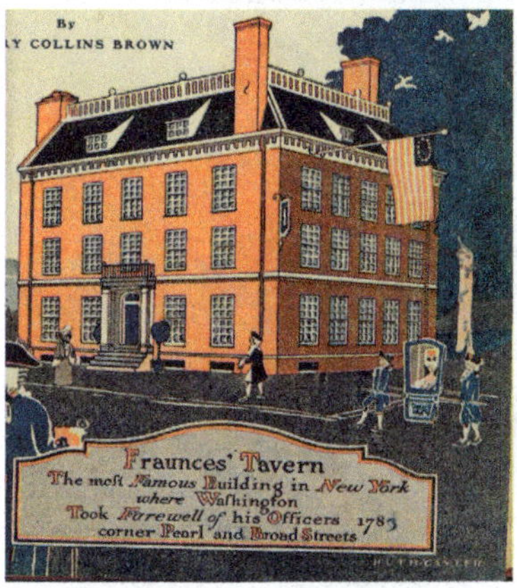

Fraunces Tavern in New York City dominated a 1920 ad by Henry Brown. The tavern, a United States landmark, is a museum and restaurant located at 54 Pearl St.

courtesy Wiki Commons

The Archives of The Gov. George Clinton papers contain a description of the farewell scene:

On Thursday noon the principal officers of the army assembled at Fraunces tavern to take a final leave of their much-loved commander in chief. After a while gen. Washington came in, and calling for a glass of wine thus addressed them: "With a heart full of love and gratitude I now take leave of you. I most devoutly wish that your latter days may be as prosperous and happy as your former, ones have been glorious and honorable." Having drank he said: " I cannot come to each of you to take my leave; but shall be obliged to you if each will come and take me by the hand." General Knox being nearest turned to him; Washington with tears rolling down his cheeks, grasped Knox's hand and then kissed him: he did the same by every succeeding officer, and by some other gentlemen who were present. The passions of human nature were never more tenderly agitated, than in this interesting and distressful scene. The whole company were in tears. When Washington left the room, and passed through the corps of light infantry about two o'clock on his way to Whitehall the others followed, walking in a solemn, mute and mournful procession, with heads hanging down and dejected countenances, till he embarked in his barge. When he had entered, he turned, took off his hat, and with that bid them a silent adieu.

"Washington's Farewell to His Officers," Alonzo Chappel, 1866 courtesy Wiki Commons.

Washington came to Congress at Annapolis on Dec. 23, 1783, to resign his commission painting, by John Trumbull, courtesy Wiki Commons.

Spring 1798, Washington Irving: To help 15-year old Washington Irving escape an outbreak of yellow fever, his parents sent him up the Hudson River from Manhattan to Tarrytown, about 13 miles south of Anthony's Nose. While staying at Tarrytown, he would visit neighboring Sleepy Hollow, came to love the area, and eventually moved there. In 1800, his parents again sent him north to avoid disease, a tuberculosis outbreak. He rode on a sloop that traveled up the Hudson River, past Anthony's Nose, the Highlands, and the Catskill Mountains to Albany and then on to Johnstown.

Washington Irving;
Library of Congress

Another influence on Washington Irving was George Washington, whom he was named and whom he met in person when he was 6 years old. Washington had just been inaugurated as president and was living in New York City.

Watercolor by George Bernard Butler
Of Washington Irving's encounter with
George Washington.
courtesy Wiki Commons

A prolific writer, Washington Irving had a long, successful career both in the United States and Europe, where he lived for many years, and coined New York City terms still used today, such as Knickerbockers and Gotham.

In 1835 Irving bought a run-down cottage and surrounding land on the Hudson River near Tarrytown. He named the cottage Sunnyside, continued to make improvements to the estate, and after extensive traveling, made it his home for life. Sunnyside is now open for tours as a National Historic Site.

Irving's Sunnyside, on The Hudson River, became one of the best known and often-visited estates in the country.

courtesy Wiki Commons

The Hudson Valley influenced some of Irving's most famous works. "The legend of Sleepy Hollow" was inspired by a Hessian soldier decapitated by a cannonball (At Hessian Lake, across from Anthony's Nose, many Hessians were killed during the battle of Fort Montgomery).

John Quidor's painting of the Headless Horseman pursuing Ichabod Crane; courtesy Wiki Commons

Another of Irving's most famous short stories was "Rip Van Winkle," about a Dutch, Colonial American who falls asleep in the Catskill mountains for 20 years and wakes up missing the Revolutionary War and the drastic changes that occurred.

John Quidor's painting of Rip Van Winkle; courtesy Wiki Commons

Irving also wrote about Anthony's Nose in his *"Knickerbocker's History of New York," stating that* Anthony Van Corlaer, the trumpeter of New Amsterdam, had an enormous shiny red nose.

Painting of trumpeter Anthony Van Corlaer, by Charles Loring, from Walters Art Museum; courtesy Wiki Commons

Summer 1799, early gristmill: Eugene Lucet built a gristmill on the Popolopen Creek, across the Hudson from Anthony's Nose, a location that allowed access to the River. The mill brought in stores, houses, docks, and later a sawmill. Grist is grain, such as corn or wheat, that has been separated from its casing and is ready for grinding. The mill uses the flow of water to turn a vertical wheel (usually wooden) to grind the grist against a millstone and produce cornmeal and flour or cereal. Mills go back thousands of years, progressing over time, and are considered one of the greatest inventions, saving labor and time.

Old postcard of Lucet Mill on Popolopen Creek

The miller would charge a "miller's toll" of usually 10% of the flour or ground meal. He would keep some and sell or barter some for other products or work. The Europeans brought the original mill technology to America. The sawmill was another type of mill that would easily turn logs into boards for building furniture, houses, fences etc.

After Eugene Lucet built his mill, there was a property dispute about ownership of the mill land. Lucet needed a lawyer, so he hired Alexander Hamilton to help win his case.

In the Hamilton Papers, Library of Congress, there are three enclosures in Lucet's handwriting which are entitled:

"statement relative to the suit of Wm Donaldson vs. E. Lucet tending to eject him from the possession of his property on Puplopes Kill;

Replica of an old mill

During the Revolutionary War mills were important and necessary to feed the troops.

From George Washington to Major Gen. Nathanael Greene, 29 Oct. 1778:

There are good Barracks at Trenton and Burlington, and the adjacent Country abounding in Wheat and Mills to manufacture it. All the troops stationed there being fed upon the spot

Over time mills were located everywhere there was running water; if not, a dam was built to cause water to flow. Some of the remnants like Luccet's mill still exist today. Many towns, street names, and historical buildings have mill in their names.

Aug. 17, 1807, The world's first successful steamboat: The North River Steamboat (also called The Clermont) sailed past Anthony's Nose after leaving New York City en route to Albany. The Clermount was invented by Robert Fulton and financed by Robert Livimgston.

The Clermont leaving the dock in New York City.
courtesy Wiki Commons

Robert Fulton, an inventor born in Pennsylvania, was 42 years old when he built the Clermont. Fulton had invented the first practical submarine called the Nautilus, for Napoleon Bonaparte, leader of France. Fulton also had a passion for steam engines.

Robert Livingston, born in New York City, was 61 years old at the time of the Clermont. Both his father and mother (Beekman) were from wealthy families. Robert was a lawyer, politician, diplomat and one of the Founding Fathers who helped draft the Declaration of Independence. He lived at his estate Clermont Manor on the Hudson River in Columbia County.

The two met in France when Livingston was the U.S. ambassador to France in 1801. They experimented with different designs and while in France created a steamboat. They tested the boat in the Seine River and it sank. This did not stop the pair and they soon collaborated to build the Clermont in New York.

As with any new idea, there were many skeptics and the boat was called "Fulton's Folly."

Old postcard of Clermont

The first trip left New York City on Aug. 17, 1807, at 9 a.m. The steamboat traveled up the Hudson River north past Anthony's Nose and stopped at Livingston's Clermont estate for 20 hours and then proceeded to Albany. The total travel time was 32 hours. On the first trip there were many dignitaries, including Fulton himself. While on the trip he announced his engagement to Harriet Livingston, a relative of Robert Livingston.

The passengers, dressed in typical suits and dresses, experienced a few problems that eventually were corrected with future enhancements. Clermont's steam engine was loud and the billowing black smoke smelled; it blew in their faces depending on the wind direction and also adhered to their clothes. The two original paddle wheels (one on each side) did not have covers, so fish, driftwood and river water went up in the air and landed on the passengers that were on the ships deck and had to be cleaned off regularily. Most were still excited about being on the first historical voyage. The crowds on the shore complained of the noise and the smoke. The trip was a success, at 5 miles an hour it went past the sloops and was not dependent on wind availability.

Robert Livingston was able to get a 20-year exclusive monopoly on Hudson River steamboats and soon had continuous service between New York City and Albany with stops along the way.

From *Old Steamboat Days on the Hudson*, 1907 from the Library of Congress:

It cost something to travel by steamboat those days, but the boat didn't lack patronage. There was no fare less than $1.00 for any fraction of twenty miles. From New York to Verplanck's Point it was $2.00, West Point, $2.50, Newburg, $3.00, Wappingers Creek, $3.25, Poughkeepsie, $3.50, Hudson, $5.00, and Albany, $7.00.

Over time the steamboat was used throughout the world including on the Mississippi River. The Hudson River alone had over 50 steamboats traveling between New York and Albany, including ferry steamboats.

Clermont replica built for the 100th year anniversary
Library of Congress

In time there were many postcards and models of the Clermont.

Vintage *Anthony's Nose postcard*

1820 -1861: The Underground Railroad route to safety: One of the common sections of a route to safety to Canada was along the Hudson River between New York City and Albany via train, steamships, sloops or barges that all traveled past Anthony's Nose.

The Underground Railroad was a metaphor describing the secret travel routes, methods, and safe houses used to help slaves flee to free sections of the country and Canada. Over 100,000 slaves used the Underground Railroad to escape. The network of allies that ran the Underground Railroad included abolitionists (like Harriet Tubman and Fredrick Douglass), Quakers, churches against slavery, and many citizens who helped directly or through donations. Anyone involved in the Underground Railroad was at risk from slave catchers whose efforts became easier when Congress passed the *Fugitive Slave Act. A* federal law, it required free states to recapture runaway slaves and made federal agents enemies of the Underground Railroad. Newspapers also participated in helping recapture slaves by publishing ads that offered generous rewards for seizing and returning escaped slaves. This encouraged bounty hunters, who on occasion would capture free African American men, women and children and sell them to southern slave owners.

TWO HUNDRED DOLLARS

REWARD!

Ran away from the subscriber, on the 6th inst., my boy Manuel. He is about 35 years of age, about 5 feet 7 inches high, heavy built weighing about 160 pounds. He has a shrewd expression of the eye, and has a scar on one of his thighs occasioned from a burn, is well dressed and has in his possession a figured plush carpet-bag.

I will give a Reward of $200 for the apprehension and delivery of said boy at my house about ten miles from Berry's Ferry, or in the Livingston county Jail, if taken in any other State; or $50 if taken within the State of Kentucky. E. M. DULEY.

Livingston Co., Ky., May 9, 1860.

This ad in 1860 is an example of the many that encouraged bounty hunters. $200 dollars in 1860 is equivalent to $7,181 today. The ad mentions that any state (even free states) can capture Manuel and bring him back to get the reward. Since federal laws were on the side of the slave catcher, the Underground Railroad was, in many cases, the only chance a slave had to obtain freedom.

This ad was from a story by Enoch Duley in the Gilder Lehrman Institute of American History.

In this book, In Defiance, *by New Paltz historians Susan Stessin-Cohn and Ashley Hurlburt-Biagini, the authors feature 523 actual Hudson Valley ads for runaway slaves.*

In 1838, while in London, Moses Roper wrote the *Adventures and Escape of Moses Roper from American Slavery*. Moses, who went on to become a noted lecturer in England, describes his escape from terrible slave masters. The trip included being on board an old schooner named Fox that traveled from New York City past Anthony's Nose and stopped in Poughkeepsie.

Moses Roper, shown in 1846, was an escaped slave who was helped by the Underground Railroad.

courtesy Wiki Commons

Below are excerpts from Moses's book describing his experience after he got off the schooner in Poughkeepsie. Moses mentions at the end of the book that he was careful not to mention the name of any person who could thus be identified and face arrest. Along the way he was helped and warned of danger by a network of Underground Railroad patrons.

"I then returned to New York; but finding the same difficulty there to get work, as in the country, I went back to the vessel, which was to sail eighty miles up the Hudson River, to Poughkeepsie. When I arrived, I obtained employment at an inn, and after I had been there for about two days, I was seized with the cholera, which was at that place. The complaint was, without doubt, brought on by my having subsisted on fruit only, for several days while I was in the slave states. The landlord of the inn came to me when I was in bed, suffering violently from cholera, and told me he knew I had that complaint, and as it had never been in his house, I could not stop there any longer. No one would enter my room, except a young lady, who appeared very pious and amiable, and had visited persons with the cholera. She immediately procured me some medicine at her own expense, and administered it herself; and, whilst I was groaning with agony, the landlord came up and ordered me out of the house directly. Most of the persons in Poughkeepsie had retired for the night, and I lay under a shed on some cotton bales.

The medicine relieved me, having been given so promptly; and next morning I went from the shed, and laid on the banks of the river below the city. Towards evening, I felt much better, and went on in a steam-boat, to the city of Albany, about eighty miles. When I reached there, I went into the country, and tried for three or four days to procure employment, but failed. At that time, I had scarcely any money, and lived upon fruit, so I returned to Albany, where I could get no work, as I could not show the recommendations I possessed, which were only from slave states, and I did not wish anyone to know. I came from them. After a time, I went up the western canal, as a steward, in one of the boats. When I had gone about 350 miles up the canal, I found I was going too much towards the slave states, in consequence of which, I returned to Albany, and went up the northern canal, into one of the New-England States, Vermont. The distance I had traveled, including the 350 miles I had to return from the west, and the 100 to Vermont...I found people very hospitable and kind, they seemed opposed to slavery, so I told them I was a runaway slave. I hired myself to a firm in Sudbury.

After I had been in Sudbury some time, the neighboring farmers told me, that I had hired myself for much less money than I ought. I mentioned it to my employers, who were very angry about it; I was advised to leave by some of the people round, who thought the gentlemen I was with would write to my former master, informing him where I was, and obtain their ward fixed upon me.

*Fearing I should be taken, I immediately left, and went into the town of Ludlow, where I met with a kind friend, Mr.———————— *who sent me to school for several weeks and was. At this time, I was advertised in the papers obliged to leave; I went a little way out of Ludlow to a retired place, and lived two weeks, and weeks with a Mr. ———— deacon of a church at Ludlow; at this place, I could have obtained education, had it been safe to have remained. From there, I went to New Hampshire, where I was not safe, so I went to Boston, Massachusetts, with the hope of returning to Ludlow, to which place, I was much attached. At Boston, I met with a friend, who kept a shop, and took me to assist him for several weeks. Here I did not consider myself safe, as persons from all parts of the country were continually coming to the shop,and I feared, some might come who knew me.....*

*Note: * It would not be proper to mention any names,as a person in any of the States in America, found harboring a slave,would have to pay a heavy fine.*

The Underground Railroad continued until President Lincoln signed the Emancipation Proclamation and the Civil War was won by the free northern states.

Nov. 22, 1825: The Hudson River School of artists. For over 50 years, landscape painters from numerous places came to the Hudson Valley. The paintings were influenced by the Romanticism style and reflect America in the 19th century in realistic and detailed works revealing the natural beauty of the Hudson Valley and, eventually, other areas.

Thomas Cole, an Englishman, was the founder of the art movement. In 1825 he rode a steamship up the Hudson River, past Anthony's Nose and stopped at West Point. He hiked the mountains and created a landscape painting that was soon published in the *New York Evening Post*. The brilliant fall colors and the beautiful landscape of the Hudson Valley soon became known throughout the world. About 25 notable artists were Hudson River School members. Many of the valuable artworks are exhibited all over the globe. Below are three examples:

View Near Anthony's Nose, William Bartlett, 1839
courtesy Wiki Commons

Hudson River at Croton Point, Julie Beers, Hudson River Artist, 1869; courtesy Wiki Commons

Winter Twilight from Olana (his home on the Hudson), By Frederic Edwin Church, 1871; courtesy Wiki Commons

July 1830 - March 1831: Edgar Allan Poe entered the Military Academy at West Point. Edgar Allan Poe was 21 years old and had just finished two years of a five-year assignment in the Army. He was successful and reached the highest ranking he could achieve, a sergeant major of the artillery. With influence from his guardian "stepfather," John Allan, he was able to get a coveted acceptance to West Point as a cadet.

Edgar Allan Poe
courtesy Wiki Commons

Edgar Allan Poe was well educated. He was an orphan at an early age after his father, an actor, abandoned the family and his mother, also an actor, died from tuberculosis. Edgar had a brother and sister and the three were split up and John Allan, a wealthy merchant, and his wife, took care of Edgar and sent him to fine schools around the world. Edgar did not always get along with his guardian and was always trying to become independent and out of his stepfather's control. The military was a way to do this and also to gain respect from his grandfather, David Poe, who was an admired quartermaster during the Revolutionary War and is mentioned in letters to George Washington.

In the beginning of his tenure, Edgar did really well. Soon though he started to dislike the discipline and also started to write more. When he attempted to leave the academy he found out the only way out was to stop going to class and disobey orders until he was court-martialed and expelled. Some of his fellow cadets supported his writing future and they collected money to help him publish a poem.

William James Bennett, 1830. courtesy Wiki Commons

This painting is of West Point, from the south at Philipstown. The painting was created during the period Edgar Allan Poe was living along the Hudson River at West Point.

Some of Poe's writing was influenced by the mountains and Hudson River Valley from his time at West Point. A line in the "Culprit Fay" says "the moon looks down on old cronest." Crowsnest is a ledge adjacent to West Point.

Searches of his work show that Poe references "mountains" 124 times and "rivers" 157 times.

Example: *immense river, mighty river, majestic river,* etc. The Hudson River is all of these.

In his "Criticism," Poe writes:

"Thence spring immediately admiration of the fair flowers, the fairer forests, the bright valleys and rivers and mountains of the Earth..."

Edgar Allan Poe died mysteriously at the age of 40 in Baltimore after being found unconscious on the street.

Summer 1843: Harriet Jacobs, an escaped slave, was on the steamship Knickerbocker on a trip up the Hudson River to Saratoga working as a nanny. The ship sailed past Anthony's Nose about half way to Saratoga. Harriet was hiding from Dr. Norcom, the person she had escaped from who was in New York looking for her and placing ads in newspapers to entice bounty hunters.

The Steamship Knickerbocker, which Harriet Jacobs was on during her trip from New York city up the Hudson River to Saratoga, appears in an old postcard.

Harriet Jacobs went on to write one of the most influential and thought-provoking books of her generation and has been recently rediscovered.

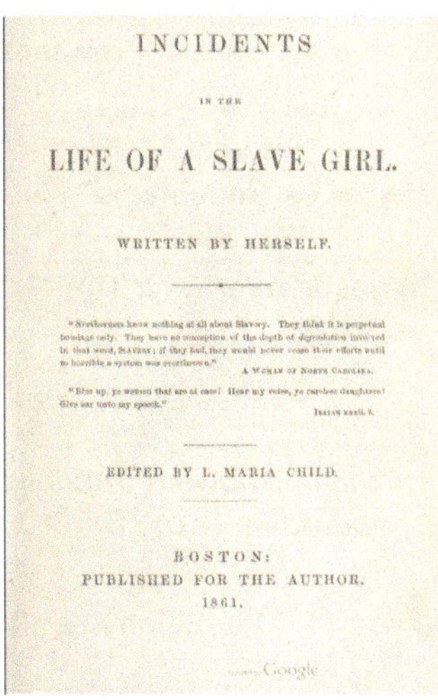

INCIDENTS

IN THE

LIFE OF A SLAVE GIRL.

WRITTEN BY HERSELF.

"Northerners know nothing at all about Slavery. They think it is perpetual bondage only. They have no conception of the depth of degradation involved in that word, SLAVERY; if they had, they would never cease their efforts until so horrible a system was overthrown."

A WOMAN OF NORTH CAROLINA.

"Rise up, ye women that are at ease! Hear my voice, ye careless daughters! Give ear unto my speech."

ISAIAH xxxii. 9.

EDITED BY L. MARIA CHILD.

BOSTON:
PUBLISHED FOR THE AUTHOR.
1861.

Harriet Jacobs autobiography, *Life Of A Slave Girl*, published in 1861, is available free on Google Books.

An excerpt from the work of Harriet Jacobs, who used the pseudonym Linda Brent to hide her identity, appears below. This excerpt describes part of her trip to Saratoga, New York.

It was a relief to my mind to see preparations for leaving the city. We went to Albany in the steamboat Knickerbocker. When the gong sounded for tea, Mrs. Bruce said, "Linda, it is late, and you and baby had better come to the table with me." I replied, "I know it is time baby had her supper, but I had rather not go with you, if you please. I am afraid of being insulted." "O no, not if you are with me," she said. I saw several white nurses go with their ladies, and I ventured to do the same. We were at the extreme end of the table. I was no sooner seated, than a gruff voice said, "Get up! You know you are not allowed to sit here." I looked up, and, to my astonishment and indignation, saw that the speaker was a colored man. If his office required him to enforce the by-laws of the boat, he might, at least, have done it politely. I replied," I shall not get up, unless the captain comes and takes me up." No cup of tea was offered me, but Mrs. Bruce handed me hers and called for another. I looked to see whether the other nurses were treated in a similar manner. They were all properly waited on.

Next morning,when we stopped at Troy for breakfast, everybody was making a rush for the table. Mrs. Bruce said, "Take my arm, Linda, and we'll go in together." The landlord heard her, and said, "Madam, will you allow your nurse and baby to take Breakfast with my family?" I knew this was to be attributed to my complexion; but he spoke courteously, and therefore I did not mind it.

At Saratoga we found the United States Hotel crowded, and Mr. Bruce took one of the cottages beLonging to the hotel. I had thought, with gladness, of going to the quiet of the country, where I should meet few people, but here I found myself in the midst of a swarm of Southerners. I looked around me with fear and trembling, dreading to see someone who would recognize me. I was rejoiced to find that we were to stay for a short time. We soon returned to New York, to make arrangements for spending the remainder of the summer at Rockaway.

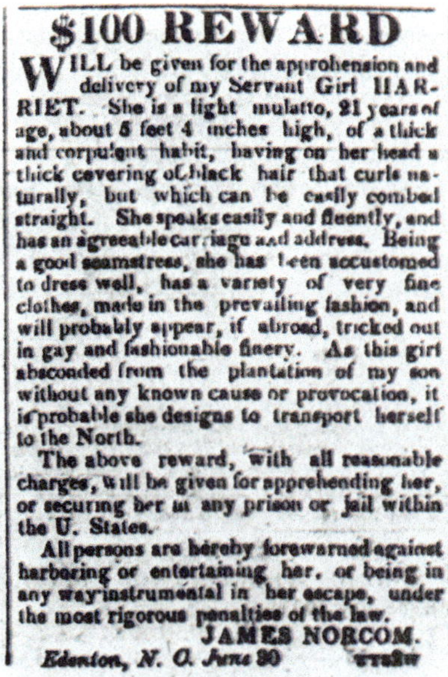

$100 REWARD

WILL be given for the apprehension and delivery of my Servant Girl HARRIET. She is a light mulatto, 21 years of age, about 5 feet 4 inches high, of a thick and corpulent habit, having on her head a thick covering of black hair that curls naturally, but which can be easily combed straight. She speaks easily and fluently, and has an agreeable carriage and address. Being a good seamstress, she has been accustomed to dress well, has a variety of very fine clothes, made in the prevailing fashion, and will probably appear, if abroad, tricked out in gay and fashionable finery. As this girl absconded from the plantation of my son without any known cause or provocation, it is probable she designs to transport herself to the North.

The above reward, with all reasonable charges, will be given for apprehending her, or securing her in any prison or jail within the U. States.

All persons are hereby forewarned against harboring or entertaining her, or being in any way instrumental in her escape, under the most rigorous penalties of the law.

JAMES NORCOM.

Edenton, N. C. June 30   TTuSW

Slave "owners" would offer rewards in newspapers around the country, including in the North, to attract bounty hunters. This is an actual ad for Harriet Jacobs from her book. The photo of Harriet is the only known photo, courtesy of Wiki Commons.

Harriet Jacobs wrote her autobiography while working for the Willis family as a nurse. A famous writer, poet and editor, Nathaniel Parker Willis owned the renowned Idlewild Estate on the Hudson River by West Point, across from Anthony's Nose. Harriet kept it a secret that she was writing in her limited spare time while working and staying in a room upstairs. She was living in an estate that was considered a writer's paradise, only the most famous book was hers. Willis worked with authors Edgar Allan Poe and Henry Wadsworth Longfellow.

June 20, 1844: The "Kidd (Captain) Salvage Company" was created to hunt for pirate Capt. William Kidd's sunken ship.

The ship supposedly sank in the Hudson River across from Anthony's Nose. A large amount of stock was soon put on the market based on speculation and folklore to lure prospects. One New Yorker invested $20,000. Fifty men were employed to look for the treasure, pursuing such tasks as damming water and installing a large noisy steam pump to clear the water away for digging. In three years of searches for the treasure, two cannons were discovered that were not identified as being from Kidd's ship. For years the site drew spectators and interest and hope from the shareholders. The only people that made any money were the owners and creator of the salvage company.

At Kidds Point and DunderBerg Point (across from Anthonys' Nose) the steam water pump (depicted here) pumped water to allow digging. The images come from an 1800s book The Hudson, The Wilderness to the Sea, *found in the Library of Congress.*

For many years after they stopped searching for Kidd's treasure, the old dam and some of the pump remained visible and appeared on local maps as a hazard for ships to avoid.

William Kidd was born in Scotland in 1645, spent 20 years working on various ships from an early age and eventually became a captain under British rule. At 37 he came to New York and soon married 20-year-old Sarah Oort, who received a large inheritance after her previous husband died. They had two children. Kidd's inner circle included governors and prominent citizens like the Livingstons.

When in New York, Kidd was hired by many prominent citizens and British royalty to catch pirates who were causing havoc for merchants and the British Navy. They commissioned a special ship called The Adventure Galley equipped with 36 cannons, 150 men, and special oars that allowed the ship to closely approach pirate ships that Kidd and his crew attacked.

Captain William Kidd Socializing in New York City, painting by Jean Ferris, 1920 courtesy Wiki Commons

During this period of "policing" the area for pirates, Kidd obtained treasure that was rumored to be buried at different islands and along the Hudson River. In 1697 Kidd had a fight with a gunner on board. Kidd hit the man with a bucket and fractured his skull. He died the next day. A few months later England charged Kidd with murder and for being a pirate. Kidd was arrested, brought back to England for trial, found guilty, and hanged.

Ship similar to Capt. Kidd's boat courtesy Wiki Commons

June 1, 1847: Cornelius Vanderbilt raced his prize steamboat, C. Vanderbilt, against the steamboat Oregon.

The race started in New York City and proceeded up the Hudson River 33 miles to Ossining, south of Anthony's Nose, and returned. Vanderbilt put the challenge in the paper and the purse was $1,000. Cornelious was his own skipper. The steamboat Oregon won the race with onlooking crowds along the Hudson River.

C. Vanderbilt Steamboat, painting by James Bard, 1847
courtesy Wiki Commons

Cornelius Vanderbilt, "The Commodore" was born May 27, 1794, in Staten Island, New York, to Cornelius van Derbilt and Phebe Hand. The younger Vanderbilt quit school at 11 to work with his father at the dock and at 16, with $100 borrowed from his mother, he started his own business, taking passengers on a ferry shared with his father. At 19 he married Sophie Johnson and they had 13 children.

Cornelius Vanderbilt at 52, painting
by Nathanael Jocelyn
courtesy Wiki Commons

When Cornelious was 23 he realized that the future of river transportation was in steamboats. To learn the trade he took a job with Thomas Gibbons as a captain and business manager. Gibbons had a wealth of experience and was also rich. He was the mayor of Savannah, Georgia; a planter, a lawyer, and a steamboat owner. Gibbons also sued to break the exclusive river steamboat rights by Ogden that was part of the original rights granted by Livingston and Fulton after their first steamboat the Clermont. Thomas Gibbons became a friend and mentor of Cornelias until he died.

With this experience, guidance, hard work, and a win-at-any-cost attitude, Vanderbilt went on to own many steamboats and eventually controlled the industry. His first steamboat run was New York to Peekskill, a route that he took over from his brother.

At 46, and a wealthy man from the success with steamboats, Vanderbilt started to invest in railroads. In 1840 he bought the New York, Providence and Boston railroad. Vanderbilt went on to take over railroads all over the East Coast, including the Hudson Valley line that traveled under Anthony's Nose. With his wealth he also invested in real estate, primarily in New York City, shipyards, and steamboat lines to Europe and California to exploit the California gold rush.

The Great Railroad Race, by James Fisk, 1870
Library of Congress

The Merrimack battle. by Louis Prang & co. Library of Congress

When the Civil War started, the famous Confederate ship the Merrimack, an ironclad, was causing problems with blocades. President Lincoln invited Vanderbilt to the White House and asked if the Union could use his C. Vanderbilt steamship to help stop the Ironclad. Vanderbilt's steamship did the job and he was awarded the Congressional Gold Medal.

Vanderbilt's favorite son and future heir died of illness at the Military Academy at West Point.

When Cornelius Vanderbilt died at 82, he was one of the richest men in the world. His estate was worth $105,000,000 (about $220 billion today). He left 95 percent of his estate to his oldest son, William. Although he lived modestly, his descendants built lavish Vanderbilt estates all over the world during the Gilded Age.

May 24, 1849, Frederick Douglass: The steamship Alida was sailing by Anthony's Nose and among those on board was 32-year-old Fredrick Douglass who was soon to give one of his many famous speeches at the New England Convention in Boston. He described his experiences:

Steamboat Alida sailing from Albany to New York, courtesy Wiki Commons

From the life and Times of Frederick Douglass, *published in 1892*

On my way down the Hudson river, from Albany to New York, at one time, on the steamer Alida, in company with some English ladies who had seen me in their own country, received and treated as a gentleman, I ventured, like any other passenger, to go, at the call of the dinner bell, into the cabin and take a seat at the table; but I was forcibly taken from it and compelled to leave the cabin. My friends, who wished to enjoy a day's trip on the beautiful Hudson, left the table with me, and went to New York hungry and not a little indignant and disgusted at such barbarism. There were influential persons on board the Alida, on this occasion, a word from whom might have spared me this indignity; but there was no ***Edward Marshall*** *among them to defend the weak and rebuke the strong.*

Who was Edward Marshall? He was a passenger Fredrick Douglass ran into on a previous steamship trip:

Many years ago, on my way from Cleveland to Buffalo on one of the lake steamers, the gong sounded for supper. There was a rough element on board, such as at that time might be found anywhere between Buffalo and Chicago. It was not to be trifled with, especially when hungry. At the first sound of the gong there was a furious rush for the table. From prudence, more than from lack of appetite, I waited for the second table, as did several others. At this second table I took a seat far apart from the few gentlemen scattered along its side, but directly opposite a well-dressed, fine-featured man of the fairest complexion, high forehead, golden hair, and light beard. His whole appearance told me he was somebody. I had been seated about a minute or two when the steward came to me and roughly ordered me away. I paid no attention to him, but proceeded to take my supper, determined not to leave unless compelled to do so by superior force, and, being young and strong, I was not entirely unwilling to risk the consequences of such a contest. A few moments passed, when on each side of my chair there appeared a stalwart of my own race. I glanced at the gentleman opposite. His brow was knit, his color changed from white to scarlet, and his eyes were full of fire. I saw the lightning flash, but I could not tell where it would strike. Before my sable brethren could execute their captain's order, and just as they were about to lay violent hands upon me, a voice from that man of golden hair and fiery eyes resounded like a clap of summer thunder. "Let the gentleman alone! I am not ashamed to take my tea with Mr. Douglass." His was a voice to be obeyed, and my right to my seat and my supper was no more disputed.

I bowed my acknowledgment to the gentleman and thanked him for his chivalrous interference, and, as modestly as I could, asked him his name. "I am Edward Marshall of Kentucky, now of California," he said.

Frederick Douglass was born in February 1818. After escaping slavery in Maryland, Douglass became a renowned leader and statesman of the abolitionist movement, dedicated to the elimination of slavery. He traveled all over the world and gave speeches about social injustice and the abolitionist movement, attracting large crowds wherever he went. Douglass wrote three autobiographies, at different periods of his life. He also supported the women's suffrage movement and died of a heart attack at 77 after attending a meeting at the National Council of Women, where he received a standing ovation.

Frederick Douglass 1879
National Archives

1861, 1862 and 1865: President Abraham Lincoln was on the train passing through the tunnel under Anthony's Nose on three very different occasions.

1851 sketch of train and Anthony's Nose tunnel by J.W. Orr.

In 1861 Abraham Lincoln was elected as the 16th president of the United States. This picture, from the Library of Congress, shows Lincoln as a presidential candidate before he grew his beard. Grace Bedell, a 12-year-old, requested Lincoln grow a beard to improve his looks–and he did. Lincoln stopped in Westfield, New York, on his way to his inauguration to thank Grace for her letter.

When Lincoln was elected president the country was in turmoil and ready for war. Seven states left the union and Lincoln's life was in jeopardy. Lincoln had to journey safely from his hometown of Springfield, Illinois, to Washington, D.C., for the presidential inauguration. He traveled with his family and heavy security and brought along William Henry Johnson, his valet.

The train trip took 10 days and went through many cities with huge crowds trying to greet him. For example, at the Kensington station in Philadelphia he was met by tens of thousands.

After traveling through the Anthony's Nose tunnel, Lincoln's train soon stopped in Peekskill, directly to the south.
Lincoln's inauguration train; Library of Congress image

The information below is from the Natural Park Service description of Lincoln's Peekskill visit:

Upon his arrival Lincoln stepped onto a baggage truck that was pulled up parallel to his train car that served as his speaking platform. From there he greeted the gathered crowd.
Lincoln Society

Feb. 19, 1861

Lincoln arrived at the Peekskill depot on South Water Street at 2: p.m. He said:

I have but a moment to stand before you to listen to and return your kind greeting. I thank you for this reception and for the pleasant manner in which it is tendered to me by our mutual friends. I will say in a single sentence, in regard to the difficulties that lie before me and our beloved country, that if I can only be as generously and unanimously sustained as the demonstrations I have witnessed indicate I shall be, I shall not fail; but without your sustaining hands I am sure that neither I nor any other man can hope to surmount those difficulties. I trust that in the course I shall pursue I shall be sustained, not only by the party that elected me, but by the patriotic people of the whole country.

The next time Lincoln passed through the Anthony's Nose tunnel on a train was June 1862, when he made an unannounced secret trip to visit the West Point Military academy and the West Point Foundry, in Cold Spring, across the Hudson River from West Point.

West Point sketch from The Hudson River, by D. Appleton and Co., 1888. Found in the Library of Congress.

The trip away from Washington lasted three days. The president only selected two people to travel with him, William Henry Johnson, his valet, and Daniel McCallum, director of Military Records. The Civil War was not progressing that well for the Union Army so Lincoln was seeking changes. Lincoln wanted to meet with military leaders at West Point to plan strategy; he also toured the West Point Foundry to see the new Parrott cannon. Robert Parrott, who created the cannon in 1860, demonstrated the power of the weapon, used in the Battle of Gettysburg and in other battles, starting in spring 1861.

10-pounder Parrott rifle at Little Round Top, Gettysburg National Military Park

After the West Point trip, the president made many changes that eventually led to The Union Army's victory.

The last time Lincoln passed through the tunnel under Anthony's Nose was after he was assassinated and the funeral train carried his body back to Springfield, Illinois.

Below are three pictures, from the Library of Congress, of President Lincoln's funeral train and crowds.

On April 21, 1865, the funeral train left Washington and traveled through 7 states, never exceeding 20 miles an hour.

Millions of Americans viewed the train on the way to Springfield. On the train were his son Robert Todd, other family members, and the body of his son William, who had died three years earlier of typhoid fever. Mrs. Lincoln was too upset to travel on the train. The 20-car train passed through the Anthony's Nose tunnel on April 24, at 1:30 p.m. The train was traveling along the Hudson line from New York City to Albany.

September, 1868: Frank Baum, the writer of The Wizard of Oz, is enrolled at the Peekskill Military Academy. The academy was near the Hudson River just a few miles south of Anthony's Nose. Frank's father thought that the structured learning at the military school would be beneficial.

As a 12-year-old, Frank Baum became a cadet at the Peekskill Military Academy. courtesy Wiki Commons

To Please a Child, a biography of Baum written by his son (also named Frank) stated:

After the freedom of Rose Lawn (the family farm), the confinement and discipline of the military academy were galling. Whenever his father visited him, Frank complained. After every vacation at home he found it more and more difficult to force himself to return to Peekskill. "I complained to my father about the brutal treatment I felt I was receiving at the school," he remarked many years later. "I said the teachers were heartless, callous and continually indulging in petty nagging. I told my father they were about as human as a school of fish."

Frank received his early education from home schooling, reading on his own, and tutors. Frank had many interests and a great desire to learn and was never afraid to adventure into a new field of study, a new occupation, or a new hobby. He also had a vivid imagination and was always creating stories.

A young Frank Baum when he ventured into acting

Frank Baum was born and raised in upstate New York. His Father, Benjamin Baum, and mother, Cynthia, had 9 children. Benjamin was a successful businessman and the family lived comfortably on a large farm. The parents were very supportive of the children and encouraged them to explore. From an early age Frank would tell stories and write plays. Frank married Maud Gage in 1882 and they had 4 sons. Although he enjoyed writing, especially children's stories that he would tell to his sons, he needed a job that would support the family.

Over the years Frank and his family traveled around the country working different jobs until he finally found success selling his children's books. In 1897, at the age of 41, he published *Mother Goose Prose* and was finally able to quit his sales job and write full time.

In 1899 he published *Father Goose* with illustrator W.W.Denslow. And the following year the same team published *The Wonderful Wizard Of OZ* that soon made Baum famous. He went on to write 14 sequels to Oz, 41 novels, 80 short stories, 200 poems and 42 scripts. poster courtesy Wiki Commons

The Wonderful Wizard of Oz continues to be one of the most successful books of all time partly thanks to the 1939 movie *The Wizard of Oz* starring Judy Garland.

March 31. 1884: Thomas Edison lit up the City of Newburgh, the first city (a small section of Manhattan was lit up the year before) to benefit from his Edison bulbs and a power plant. During the construction of the plant Edison would take the train from Manhattan up the Hudson River, past Anthony's Nose to the Beacon train station, and then take a ferry across the river to Newburgh, a small bustling city at the edge of the Hudson Highlands, north of Anthony's Nose.

A young Thomas Edison and the history marker in Newburgh, New York at the Edison Power Plant courtesy Library of Congress

Thomas Edison, who was homeschooled and never had a formal education, was a prolific inventor and held 1,093 patents. Edison was able to improve on many technologies and turned ideas into practical applications for the mass public. He also was the first person to create a corporate research center, a factory for inventions and improving on ideas to make practical use of each invention. Edison built a laboratory in Menlo Park, N.J. and hired top scientists and engineers. Improvements and patents have always been an important part of American progress. The first patent, a new method of making potash, was signed by George Washington.

Thomas Edison's lab was the predecessor to corporate research centers. Bell Labs (AT&T), Watson Research Center (IBM), Texaco Research Center (Texaco), were all local labs dedicated to ideas.

Spring 1895: A 14-year-old *Helen Keller and Miss Anne Sullivan* *(her teacher) went by Anthony's Nose on a steamship from New York City.* *In October 1894, Helen Keller had attended the Wright-Humason School for the Deaf in New York City, accompanied by Sullivan.* The school was very advanced and during her time at the school Helen studied geography, arithmetic, French and German. In her book, *The Story of My Life*, she talks about taking spring excursions to various places of interest, including trips up the Hudson River to visit West Point and Tarrytown, the home of Washington Irving, whose estate, Sleepy Hollow, she enjoyed walking through.

A young Helen Keller and Miss Anne Sulivan
From her book The Story of My Life.

These photos show t*he Wright-Humason school in New York City, and Helen Keller, seated far left, holding hands with Anne Sullivan. Courtesy the American Foundation for the Blind*

When Helen Keller was 19 months old she was sick, possibly with scarlet fever, with an extreme high fever. The sickness left her blind and deaf. After years of struggling her mother asked Alexander Graham Bell (inventor of the telephone) for advice. Sullivan was recommended and she worked with Helen continually until she had a breakthrough with the word "water" at a water pump.

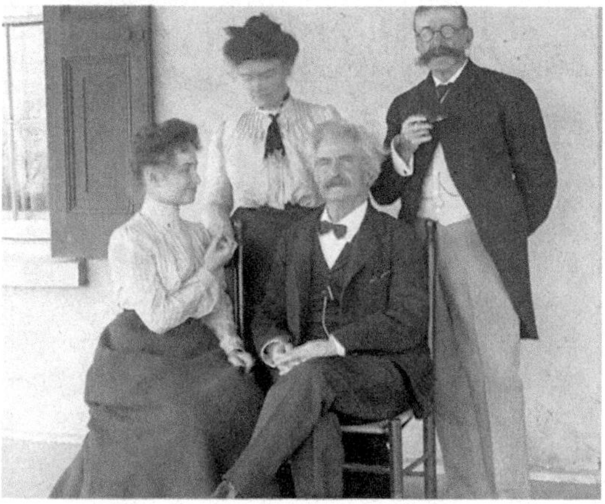

Helen and Anne with their friend Mark Twain

courtesy the American Foundation for the Blind

Over the years Helen and Anne, with the help of others, would never stop learning and exploring and became an inspiration to the world. Helen graduated from Radcliffe College in 1904 and soon became an author (14 books), and an advocate for people with disabilities. Anne Sullivan became Helen's teacher and friend when Anne was only 20 years old. Anne was partially blind and was raised in an orphanage until she was admitted to the Perkins School for the Blind. The school changed Anne's life and taught her the skills needed to teach Helen.

Anne died at the age of 70 in Queens, New York, from heart problems. Helen was there with Anne and they were holding hands when she died. The Academy Award-winning movie *The Miracle Worker*, with Patty Duke and Anne Bancroft, and a play with the same name, tell the story of Helen's incredible life.

May 29, 1910: At age 32, Glenn Hammond Curtiss breaks the long distance flying record. Curtiss flew down the Hudson River from Albany to New York City. Passing West Point, he waved to the saluting crowds below, experienced turbulence, and had to quickly descend to 40 feet over the river as he reached Anthony's Nose. Since Glenn also delivered mail, this was the world's first "airmail" flight.

Glenn Curtiss and his wife Lena Pearl in his "Hudson Flyer" biplane were photographed before the takeoff in Albany, New York. courtesy Glenn H. Curtiss Museum in Hammondsport, New York and the Library of Congress

This flight was covered by newspapers all over the country and journalists on a train followed the flight. When he reached New York City Curtiss was greeted by the mayor, thousands of people in the streets and on rooftops, and boats blowing their horns as he circled the Statue of Liberty. The total air time was 2 hours and 51 minutes. For his achievement, Curtiss also won a $10,000 prize from publisher Joseph Pulitzer (of Pulitzer Prize fame). This flight influenced more long-distance flights and started an aviation boom.

The Curtiss Museum collection includes a few firsthand observations about this flight:
When Curtiss sped past, a Catskill telegraph operator announced:

"Curtiss just went by here and he is gone, going like h _ _ _ !"
As Curtis passed the present "walkway over the Hudson" he had to decide to go under it or over it. He chose to fly over it.

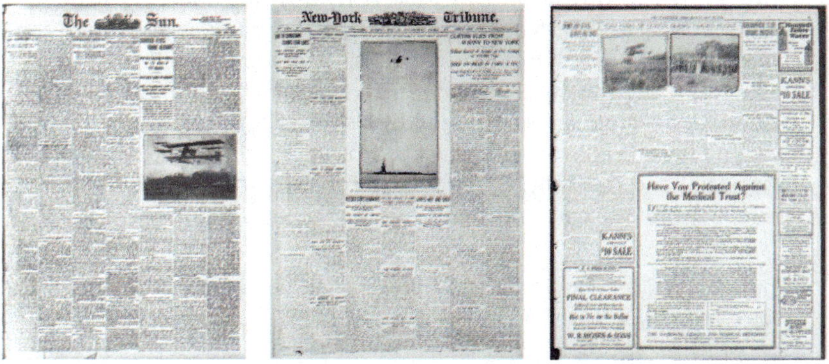
The Sun.

New-York Tribune.

Newspapers avidly covered the historic flight. Library of Congress

An aviation inventor and pioneer, Curtiss manufactured engines that he used to set land (motorcycle) and air speed records. He started the Curtiss-Wright Corporation that began building engines for the military and still exists today.

Some of his noted accomplishments:

Trained Theodore Ellyson, the first ever Navy pilot, built the first seaplane, was the first to take off from and land a plane on a ship. He also was awarded the Distinguished Flying Cross. Curtiss was on the cover of Time magazine when a stamp was issued in his name.

Library of Congress, first airmail stamp.

July 27, 1921: Franklin D. Roosevelt, 39, was honoring 2100 Boy Scouts at a Bear Mountain outing that included swimming in the lake and hosting a chicken dinner. After the event he returned to New York City. Two weeks later while vacationing at Campobello Island he became severely ill and was soon diagnosed with polio and became paralyzed from the waist down. Polio changed his life both physically and mentally. He dedicated the remainder of his life, including his years as president, to eradicating the disease.

The lake at Bear Mountain is called Hessian Lake and can be seen from Anthony's Nose.

FDR met scouts at Bear Mountain 1921. courtesy FDR Library

With his inheritance, FDR started the National Foundation for Infantile Paralysis to fight polio. The name soon became "March of Dimes" (suggested by radio DJ Eddie Cantor). FDR picked Basil O'Conner, the best person he knew to run the operation. O'Conner, who grew up poor, was highly successful at whatever business venture he started.

The country was in a panic with polio crippling hundreds of thousands of children and also causing many deaths. FDR and the March of Dimes raised millions of dollars. The March of Dimes allowed everyone to send in a dime to fight polio. Dime boxes were installed in stores, streets, restaurants, and elsewhere.

In one day, 30,000 letters came in, with dimes. Missy Lehand, FDR's secretary, was overwhelmed in a good way. courtesy Wiki Commons

FDR always spent time with polio victims. courtesy Wiki Commons

The March of Dimes funded the best lab possible and the best scientists and virologists in the world, including Jonas Salk. After 7 years including extensive testing, Salk developed a polio vaccine and was hailed as a hero throughout the country. The polio vaccine was shared around the world and said to patent the vaccine would be like patenting the sun. The March of Dimes expanded and is still successful today.

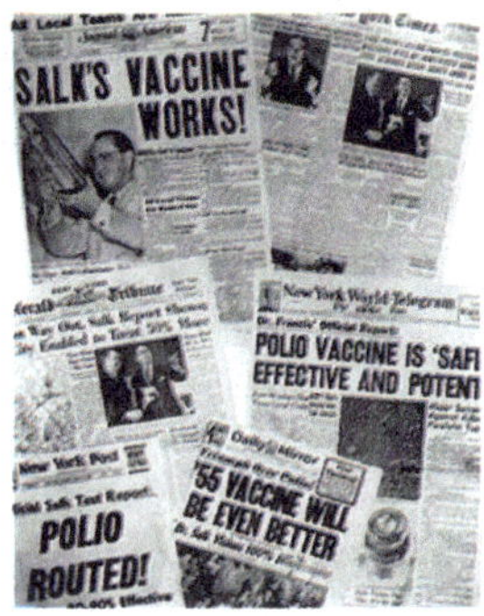

The Salk March of Dimes poster and newspapers announced the vaccine. courtesy wiki Commons

Soon after he died, the federal government changed the dime to honor Roosevelt's accomplishments, especially his establishment of, and commitment to, the March of Dimes.

FDR dime; courtesy Wiki Commons

Oct. 7, 1923: The Appalachian Trail (the AT) originated by the base of Anthony's Nose.

The first section of the trail was created starting at Bear Mountain State Park (directly on the west side of the Bear Mountain Bridge), to Harriman State Park.

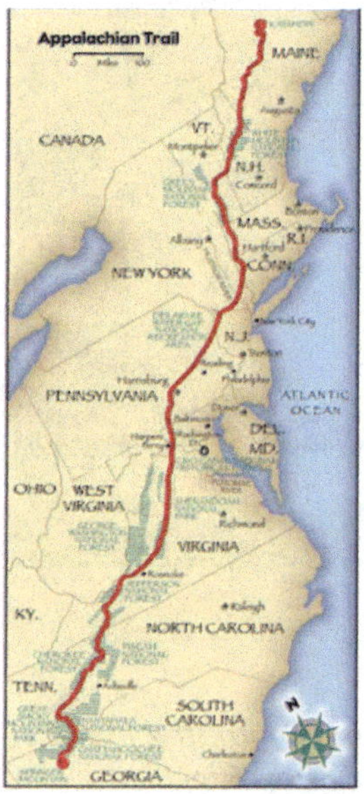

The AT is the world's most famous and longest hiking trail. The trail is 2,200 miles long and runs between Springer Mountain in Georgia to Mount Katahdin in Maine. Over 3 million people hike sections of the trail each year and over 3,000 attempt to hike the entire trail but only a quarter are successful.

Appalachian Trail logo

Benton MacKaye, a 40-year old forester, nature enthusiast from Connecticut, and Harvard graduate, conceived the trail, planned it and passionately convinced many others to help create it. MacKaye was also one of the founders of the Wilderness Society. MacKaye started working on the idea of the trail in honor of his wife, Jessie MacKaye, who loved long hikes. In 1921 Jessie died by suicide and during Benton's grieving process he published an article called "Construction of the Appalachian Trail" while staying at a friend's farm.

The Path Taken by Eric Ness details Benton MacKaye's life.

Old and new trail posters:

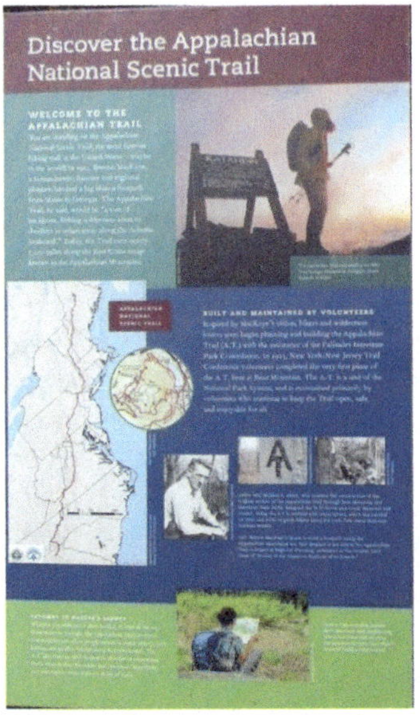

For its entire length, the famous white paint (2 by 6 inches) blaze, identifies the trail. Side trails that usually indicate a vista worth seeing are marked by blue blazes. An example is on the AT section going up to the top of Anthony's Nose.

Hikers are on the AT until close to the top of the mountain. The AT blazes continue left while a blue blaze indicates a short trail off to the right. It goes to the top of Anthony's Nose. There are more than 250 shelters of various types along the trail.

The AT became more popular in 1998 when Bill Bryson wrote *A Walk in the Woods: Rediscovering America on the Appalachian Trail.* Ten years later Robert Redford and Nick Nolte starred in the movie.

The term "trail Angel" is a term used to describe something special that occurred to someone hiking on the trail. The Appalachian Trail Conference describes a "trail angel" experience as:

Finding what you need most when you least expect it.

Experiencing something rare, extraordinary, or inspiring in nature.

Encountering unexpected acts of generosity that restore one's faith in humanity.

To become an AT "thru hiker" and hike the entire trail takes about 3-5 months. Some attempt this hike because of a life-changing event or just want to accomplish a goal. At various stages of the hike, groups will help the "thru hikers" with little things, such as passing out oranges. In Kent, Connecticut, groups sometimes have cookouts and offer lunches for "thru hikers" passing by. "Thru hikers" are very unique and always have lots of stories to tell.

Nov. 27, 1924: The Bear Mountain Bridge opened. The bridge spanned across the Hudson River between the base of Anthony's Nose and Bear Mountain State Park. The ceremonial name is the Purple Heart Veteran Memorial Bridge. At the time, the Bear Mountain bridge was the longest suspension bridge in the world and the design influenced the building of the Golden Gate Bridge and the George Washington Bridge.

Bear Mountain Bridge Construction, 1923; Library of Congress

Vintage postcard of Bear Mountain Bridge

Aug. 27, 1928: Amelia Earhart was in a small plane flying from New York City to Syracuse. The plane flew along the Hudson River past Anthony's Nose, flying low for visibility. *Earhart* had just completed her record-setting transatlantic flight on June 19, 1928. When she returned to the United States she was given a ticker tape parade in New York City and was also a guest of President Calvin Coolidge at the White House. Earhart then began a publicity tour to sites around the country, including the New York State Fair in Syracuse, New York.

1928 Syracuse Fair Program advertised Amelia Earhart as the main attraction. from Syracuse Fair archives

Amelia Earhart in LA, 1928
Los Angeles Daily News;
courtesy Wiki Commons

An article by Johnathan Croyle, *of Syracuse.com,* describes the flight up the Hudson River and what Earhart said to the thousands of waiting fans upon landing in Syracuse. (She did not personally fly that day; she was the co-pilot.)

"The flight at more than 150 feet was impossible and several times the plane was said to have flown just above the surface of the river. The fog up the Hudson reminded me more of Burry Port, Wales, where we ended our trans-Atlantic flight, than anything I have since seen," Earhart said after the plane safely landed.

After leaving the fairgrounds after four hours, she insisted she visit the Onondaga Orphanage, where she spoke and visited the excited and enthusiastic children.

Less than 9 years later, on July 2, 1937, when Amelia Earhart was 39, her plane disappeared while she was attempting to set a world flight record. Extensive searches by the U.S. Navy and privately funded groups did not find any clues to Earhart or the plane. Searches and speculations continue to this day.

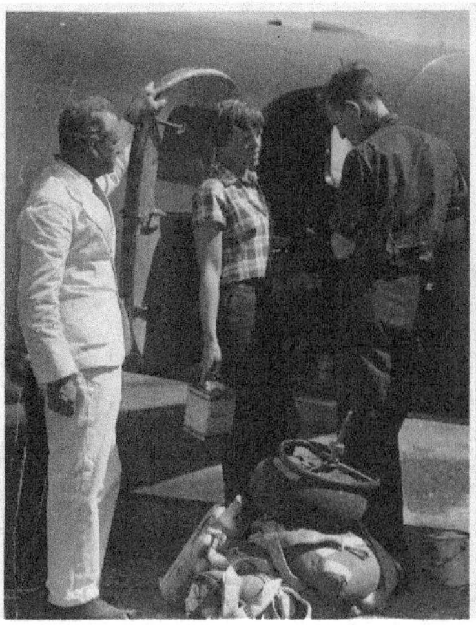

Amelia and Fred Noonan (her navigator) on June 28, prepared for what became her last flight. courtesy Wiki Commons

June 10, 1933: Eleanor Roosevelt visits Camp TERA (Temporary Emergency Relief Assistance), which she created for unemployed women. The first of many camps was called Camp Tera, and was at Bear Mountain State Park, across from Anthony's Nose. Part of the New Deal to help unemployed men after the depression was the Civilian Conservation Corps (CCC). Eleanor wanted to also help unemployed women who were left out of the CCC.

Eleanor lobbied against a lot of opposition to the idea of creating camps around the country to help women. Labor secretary Frances Perkins was behind Eleanor and supported the first camp at Bear Mountain. The camps were funded by a presidential order. In a few years 8,500 young women participated in the camps.

Eleanor Roosevelt visited the TERA Camp at Bear Mountain, Aug 7, 1933. courtesy Eleanor Roosevelt National Historic Site

At this Bear Mountain Camp Eleanor met civil rights leader Pauli Murray who enrolled there and said: "*The camp was ideal for building up run-down bodies and renewing jaded spirits.*"

"As a group women have been neglected in comparison with others," the First Lady said, "and throughout this depression have had the hardest time of all."

The above quote is from "A New Deal for Women–The She–She–She", an article published online *in The Attic.*

Below is a July 2020 article , by Erin Blakenmore, for the History Channel:

The camps were an immediate success. Most attendees reported gaining weight, learning new skills, and their surveys attested to boosts in self-esteem. "It's not only that I am getting enough to eat for the first time in three years, but I am beginning to think of myself as a real person again," one attendee wrote. Though the camps had real benefits for women, many members of the general public mocked the program. They called the program the "She-She-She" in a sendup of the CCC's initials. "She-She-She was not its name, but the men mimicked it and called it that, because women were not really people," **recalled** *labor activist Maida Smith Kemp. But despite the mockery, the program spread beyond Camp Tera, which was eventually renamed Camp Jane Addams.*

Camp for unemployed women in Oberlin, Ohio, July 1934 courtesy Wiki Commons

Oct. 19, 1936: (The "millionaire's flight") The zeppelin Hindenburg, with its red Nazi swastikas, glided 700 feet over the Hudson river and turned east below Anthony's Nose at Peekskill for a cruise over New England. Thousands came out to witness the dirigible during this journey.

Hindenburg simulation over the Hudson

The Hindenburg, the largest airship ever built, was used by Adolph Hitler and the Germans as Nazi propaganda during the Olympics and on other occasions in the 1930s.

An article in the Connecticut Magazine, Sept. 16, 2016, by Walt Sivigny describes the flight and the passenger list:

On that foggy fall morning in 1936, the Hindenburg lifted off from its U.S. docking port, the New Jersey naval station at Lakehurst, at 6:57 to the shouts of "Schiff hoch!" ("Up ship!"). The passenger list read like a who's who for 1936, which led the press to refer to it as the "Millionaires' Flight." Those on board included: Nelson Rockefeller, a 28-year-old New York financier, scion of the Rockefeller oil fortune, and future New York governor and U.S. vice president; Winthrop Aldrich, chairman of the board of Chase National Bank; Paul Litchfield, president of the Goodyear Tire & Rubber Co.; Byron Foy, an auto executive who would go on to head the Chrysler Corp.; Juan Trippe, founder of Pan American World Airways; Eddie Rickenbacker, World War I flying ace and director of Eastern Airlines; three admirals, a general, assorted government officials and a cadre of newspaper and magazine correspondents. John B. Kennedy, a reporter for NBC, was on board to provide in-flight radio broadcasts on the NBC Blue and Red networks. The only woman among these elite passengers was Mary Goodrich Jenson, a 27-year-old Wethersfield native who was the first woman to obtain a pilot's license in Connecticut. She was the aviation editor for the Hartford Courant *and the first woman to fly solo to Cuba in 1933.*

Photo taken by A.C. Langmuir, 1936

The Hindenburg blew up when landing at Lakehurst, New Jersey on May 6, 1937. The tragedy took 36 lives and ended the Zeppelin era.

Hindenburg disaster courtesy Wiki Commons.

June 11, 1939: The king and queen of England visit the United States. This was the first time any British monarchs came to America. After visiting Washington D.C., and the 1939 World's Fair in New York City, they boarded a special train that traveled past Anthony's Nose and stopped at Poughkeepsie. From Poughkeepsie, King George VI and Queen Elizabeth traveled by car to Hyde Park to meet President Franklin and Eleanor Roosevelt.

Crowds to see the king and queen at Washington, D.C., and New York City. courtesy FDR National Library, Hyde Park N.Y.

President Roosevelt invited the king and queen of England to shore up relations between the two countries and most importantly to persuade the public that England was a loyal ally of the United States. At the time, many in the U.S. advocated isolationism, the Nazis were on the verge of attacking Great Britain, and a World War was imminent. It was important that the United States support Great Britain and its allies in Europe. This trip was intended to let the Americans see the monarchs as "regular" people and not stuffy and distant.

FDR and the king in the car and the king and queen and Franklin and Eleanor Roosevelt with Sara Roosevelt (Franklin's mother) on the porch in Hyde Park. courtesy FDR Library archives

Franklin thought, although his mother Sara objected: what better way to have the king and queen be accepted than to have an outside picnic with hotdogs, strawberry shortcake and beer on the grounds of his rustic cottage in the woods. Franklin made sure to invite the press and it worked: Support for Great Britain increased.

The king sat with Sara Roosevelt, New York Gov. Herbert Lehman, Elinor Morgenthau (wife of Treasury Secretary Henry Morgenthau), the menu appears on the right. Courtesy FDR Presidential Library

MENU FOR PICNIC AT HYDE PARK

Sunday, June 11, 1939

Virginia Ham

Hot dogs ~~(if weather permits)~~

Cold turkey

Sausages (hot)

Cranberry jelly

Green salad

Rolls

Strawberry shortcake

Coffee

Beer

Soft drinks

KING TRIES HOT DOG AND ASKS FOR MORE

And He Drinks Beer With Them —Uses Own Camera to Snap Guests Photographing Him

By FELIX BELAIR Jr.

Special to THE NEW YORK TIMES.

HYDE PARK, N. Y., June 11.—King George VI ate his first hot dog, was chauffeured by the President of the United States, and turned his own hand motion-picture camera against his photographers at a typical Roosevelt picnic party today on the slope of Dutchess Hill, where the Chief Executive's new stone

LONDON SINKS TEETH INTO RESULT OF ROYAL TOUR—IT'S A HOT DOG

[Chicago Tribune Press Service.]

LONDON, June 26.—The first really tangible result of the royal visit to America—something you could sink your teeth into—made its appearance today. It was the hot dog.

This delicacy, which British aristocrats previously had scorned, has acquired a social standing of the first rank since King George VI. and Queen Elizabeth sampled it at a picnic at President Roosevelt's home.

The hot dogs had their society preview at the former home of the king and queen at 145 Piccadilly which has been opened as a museum. There the humble wieners were served amid such curios as Napoleon's shaving brush, Princess Elizabeth's cot, and Charles I.'s shirt.

London newspapers publish pictures of society belles eating the hot dogs but apparently they have not mastered the technique. They are shown holding a hot dog daintily between the thumb and forefinger.

***April 17, 1944*: Iona Island was used as a Military Munitions Site.** According to Navy archives, after completing a 10-day visit to the Brooklyn Navy Yard, the USS Daniel T. Griffon docked at the Naval Ammunition Depot at Iona Island to reload ammunition. Iona Island is located in the Hudson River across from Anthony's Nose. Over the years Iona Island has had many name changes and usages have ranged from being a summer fishing camp for Native Americans to serving as a current environmental wildlife sanctuary as part of Bear Mountain State Park. During World I and II it was used as a storage depot for ammunition since it was located in a secure location that allowed access to large ships.

The USS Daniel T. Griffin was a Buckley-class destroyer escort.

courtesy U.S.Navy photo from their archives

The Griffin was just over a football field in length, at 306 feet and had a complement of 213 men, including 15 officers. The ship was named after Daniel Thornburgh Griffin from Allendale, Illinois, who joined the Navy in 1930 at the age of 19, and was killed during the Japanese Attack on Pearl Harbor on Dec. 7, 1941. The Griffin participated in the battle of Okinawa and fought off several kamikaze suicide plane attacks and protected and helped extinguish fires when a destroyer, the Morris was hit.

The U.S. Navy owned Iona Island from 1899 until 1947. After World War II, the "mothball fleet" of ships no longer in service were moored just south of the Iona island.

Iona Island Naval Ammunition Depot and U.S. Marine Corps guard pre-1916. courtesy Palisades Interstate Park Commision.

Native Americans inhabited Iona Island (they called it Wanakawaghkin, meaning good land) until it was purchased in 1963 by the Van Cortlands, who called it Salisbury Island. Many artifacts have been found on the island, some on display at the Bear Mountain trail side museum.

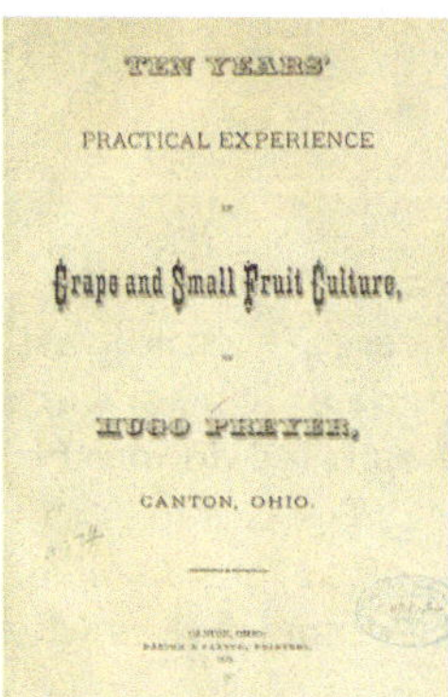

TEN YEARS'

PRACTICAL EXPERIENCE

Grape and Small Fruit Culture,

HUGO PHEYER,

CANTON, OHIO.

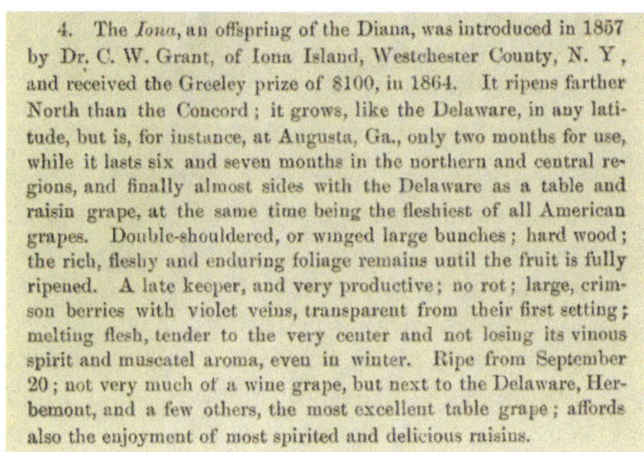

4. The *Iona*, an offspring of the Diana, was introduced in 1857 by Dr. C. W. Grant, of Iona Island, Westchester County, N. Y, and received the Greeley prize of $100, in 1864. It ripens farther North than the Concord; it grows, like the Delaware, in any latitude, but is, for instance, at Augusta, Ga., only two months for use, while it lasts six and seven months in the northern and central regions, and finally almost sides with the Delaware as a table and raisin grape, at the same time being the fleshiest of all American grapes. Double-shouldered, or winged large bunches; hard wood; the rich, fleshy and enduring foliage remains until the fruit is fully ripened. A late keeper, and very productive; no rot; large, crimson berries with violet veins, transparent from their first setting; melting flesh, tender to the very center and not losing its vinous spirit and muscatel aroma, even in winter. Ripe from September 20; not very much of a wine grape, but next to the Delaware, Herbemont, and a few others, the most excellent table grape; affords also the enjoyment of most spirited and delicious raisins.

Old books in the Library of Congress described the grapes that originated in Iona Island.

Iona grapes are sold today and were also crossed with others to create varieties like the Daimon grape used to make wines and juices.

Before the Navy purchased Iona in 1899, the most common usage of the island was for leisure activities for travelers from New York City to enjoy the beauty of the Hudson Highlands. A summer resort was built by a group of investors who also added a small amusement park and a dock for steamships to accommodate tourists. The old postcard of U.S. government structures on Iona Island shows remnants of the resort building.

In 1965 Iona Island was purchased by the Palisades Interstate Park Commission and is now a wildlife sanctuary with limited tours sponsored by the Park Commision

Spring 1945 and 1946: A major league baseball team, the Brooklyn Dodgers, held their spring training camp at Bear Mountain State Park. Because of the travel restrictions of World War II, all sports teams who usually travel south for warmer weather, had to find practice facilities close to home. Bear Mountain State Park had three baseball fields that could be seen from Anthony's Nose.

Dodgers at Bear Mountain and Leo Durocher (Dodger manager) met with owners and press courtesy Bear Mountain State Park archives

The following year, 1947, this Brooklyn Dodger team that had practiced at Bear Mountain signed Jackie Robinson, the first black baseball player allowed to play on a Major League Baseball team. Before 1947, black players were only allowed to play in Negro League teams. Branch Rickey, the Dodgers president, had been planning and searching for black players to sign for a couple of years. It wasn't possible until baseball Commissioner Kenesaw Landis, who was opposed to integration, died in 1944.

Before Jackie Robinson was signed, the first two Negro League players to ever try out for a major league team came to Bear Mountain on April 6, 1945. Although the tryouts were not planned by the Dodgers, they occurred. Joe Bostic, a sports editor for a Harlem newspaper, arrived at Bear Mountain with two Negro League players, Dave Thomas and Terris McDuffie. Both were excellent players with years of experience and success but were past their prime playing days.

After hours of pressure and determination, Branch Rickey reluctantly agreed to give them a tryout, which Rickey observed. Although he saw signs of talent he said he was not that impressed and never signed either one.

According to Chris Lamp of ESPN, who investigated this event, with new details uncovered, Joe Bostic reported as follows after the Bear Mountain incident:

"Today's extensive tryout, given Terris McDuffie and Dave Thomas by the Dodgers, represents a constructive and significant step in the effort to have Negro players in the major leagues. I feel it represents the first concrete step toward realization of that goal."

On Aug. 28, 1945, Rickey of the Dodgers met with Jackie Robinson and signed him soon after, breaking the color barrier.

Jackie Robinson participated in a publicity picture while at a conference at Bear Mountain Aug. 15, 1949. The football players are Scott Emerson from Navy and Goble Bryant (left) from Army, who were training for the college all-star game against the Giants at the Polo Grounds in New York.

photo from Library of Congress archives

Summer 1957: Neil Diamond attends Surprise Lake Camp near Cold Spring New York. Neil, 16 years old, lived in Brooklyn at the time. Surprise Lake Camp was a Jewish summer camp located on the other side of Breakneck Mountain several miles north of Anthony's Nose. In his biography and in many interviews over the years, Diamond always gave credit to Pete Seeger, the famous folk song performer, for inspiring him to write songs and be a performer.

Pete Seeger 1955
Library of Congress archives

Seeger was a neighbor and a friend of the Surprise Lake Camp. Pete and his wife, Toshi, lived in a cabin in the mountains close by and he was invited to perform there many times. During Seeger's performance he always got the kids involved with singing and writing their own songs. There were always stories floating around that Pete and Toshi would help hikers from the summer camp get back safely if they were lost.

Surprise Lake Camp is still active and popular today.

After the summer experience, Diamond, who had a guitar his parents paid off a $1 at a time, started to write his own songs. One of the most famous was "Sweet Caroline." Today "Sweet Caroline," sung today with fan participation (like Seeger encouraged) at sporting events all over the world. After the Boston Marathon bombing, Diamond personally performed this song with crowd participation, in an emotional tribute.

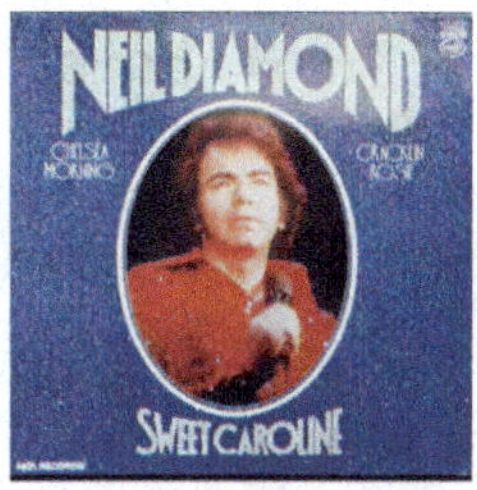

In Boston, Neil Diamond sang "Sweet Caroline," whose album cover appears, right.

One of the most successful singers and songwriters of all time, Diamond has sold more than 130 million records and had 10 No. 1 hits. He was inducted into the Rock & Roll Hall of Fame in 1984 and with many Grammys also received the Grammy Lifetime Achievement Award.

In a New York Times article, July, 20, 1986 by Stephen Holden, he interviewed Neil Diamond who said this about Pete Seeger:
''It all started with Pete Seeger,'' Mr. Diamond recalled. ''He was my original idol. I was a kid at Surprise Lake Camp, and Pete came up to give us kids a demonstration and to play some songs. It was basically a folk show where he got everybody singing along and having a good time. If I patterned my stage approach after anything, it had to be that, because the audience was part of the show. He also inspired me as a songwriter. The first songs I ever learned were on the Weavers' albums. Ten years ago, I bumped into Pete in a restaurant and was amazed to discover that he knew who I was. I said, 'You've had more of an influence on my life that you could ever possibly imagine - you're my hero.' ''

June 19, 1961: Bob Dylan wrote the song "*Talkin Bear Mountain Picnic Massacre Blues.*"

For over a 100 years, travelers from New York City booked day trips on Hudson River steamships. Over the years millions of passengers boarded these for excursions to riverside parks, including Bear Mountain State Park.

One of the Hudson River steamships that traveled from New York to Bear Mountain was the Hudson Belle.

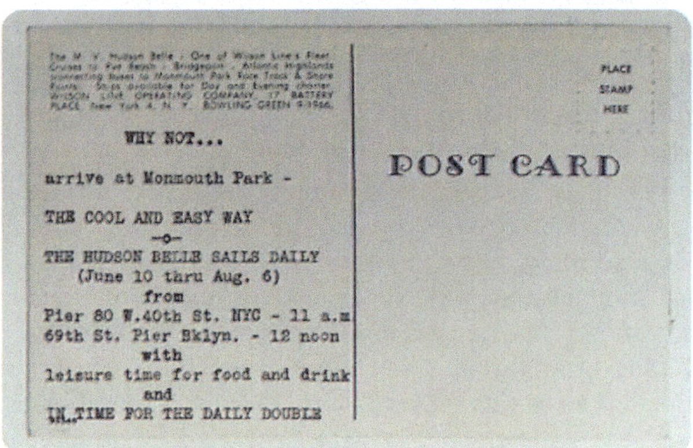

Postcard of the Hudson Belle in NYC

The Bear Mountain dock can be seen from Anthony's Nose.

Bear Mountain Dock used for day-liners

In 1961, The Harlem Social Club hired the Hudson Belle steamship for a Father's Day picnic trip to Bear Mountain. Many tickets were fraudulently copied, causing more people to attempt to board than the Belle could accommodate. Fights broke out, 20 people were injured and the Belle never did sail to Bear Mountain. The New York Herald Tribune printed an article on the abandoned boat trip. Paul Stookey, later of the Peter, Paul and Mary band, read the article and gave it to 20-year-old Bob Dylan, who was performing in the Gaslight Cafe with Stookey. The next day Dylan came in with a song inspired by the article.

The humorous song was called "Talkin Bear Mountain Picnic Massacre Blues" and Dylan would sing it many times before he was signed by Columbia Records.

Dylan is considered by many to be one of the greatest songwriters of all time and has sold more than 120 million albums. He received the Medal of Freedom in 2012 and the Nobel Prize in Literature in 2016, plus 10 Grammy Awards, and was inducted in the Rock & Roll Hall of Fame, as well as being honored by numerous awards around the world.

Nov. 9, 1965: Frances "Franny" Reese helped spearhead a grassroots campaign that led to the decision by the 2nd U.S. Circuit Court of Appeals in New York stopping the Consolidated Edison power plant from being built on Storm King Mountain. Storm King is in the Highlands and can be seen from Anthony's Nose.

This decision had monumental effects on future environmental debates throughout the country and was the start of the environmental non profit Scenic Hudson.

Franny Reese (1917-2003) helped save Storm King Mountain, across the river from here. She spent over 40 years keeping the Hudson Valley beautiful.

Scenic Hudson Archives

ScenicHudson.org

A Franny Reese quote form Scenic Hudson:

Scenic Hudson says: "We continue to be inspired by the credo of Scenic Hudson co-founder Frances 'Franny' Reese: 'Care enough to take action. Do your research so you don't have to backtrack from a position. And don't give up!' "

Scenic Hudson has continued to protect and enhance the Hudson Valley by creating and enhancing parks, including the Franny Reese Park in Highland, New York, and strongly advocate environmental policies.

June 24, 1967: Young Don McLean, who lived in the area, borrowed his mother's car and crossed the Bear Mountain Bridge below Anthony's Nose, to see Pete Seeger perform at a folk festival in Garrison, New York. McLean would go on to become one of the most famous singer-songwriters in history, penning classics, including *"American Pie," "Vincent,"* and *"Empty Chairs."*

In an in-depth article in a local newspaper, *The Highlands Current,* Alison Rooney details McLean's early days living in the Highlands and the influence the area had on his career, including its connections to Pete Seeger and other folk singers. McLean lived in Philipstown, and would ride horses in the Highlands by Anthony's Nose, and spend time with Seeger while working on his craft.

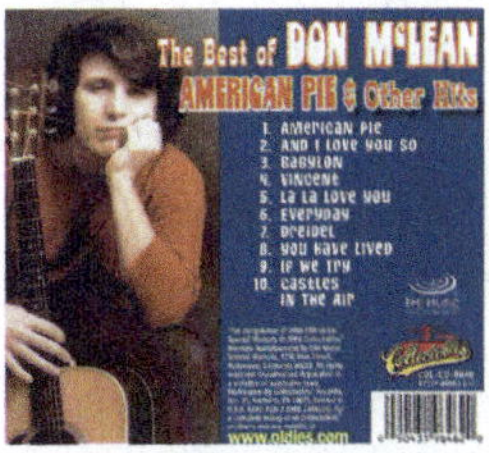

Don McLean and an album cover of his greatest hits

In 1971, McLean released "American Pie" and it soon became a Chart-topping song worldwide for many weeks. Over the years "American Pie" has been featured by many top artists, and used in many movies, and is considered one of the most successful and talked-about songs of all time. The phrase in the song "when the music dies" refers to a plane crash that killed pioneering rock 'n' roll stars Buddy Holly, Ritchie Valens and The Big Bopper.

McLean's song *"Vincent,"* on the same album as "American Pie," was a tribute to Vincent Van Gogh. The famous first phrase in the song, "Starry, Starry Night," referred to Van Gogh's painting of the same name. Songwriter Lori Lieberman said that McLean's *"Empty Chairs"* was the influence for *"Killing Me Softly With His Song"* a No. 1 hit by Roberta Flack.

May 17, 1969: Pete Seeger launched the sloop Clearwater which sailed up the Hudson River, past Anthony's Nose, to its home in the Hudson Valley. After a successful folk singer-songwriting career, in 1966, Pete and his wife Toshi started the Hudson River Sloop Clearwater, a non-profit organization that started in Poughkeepsie, New York, and eventually moved to Beacon. The mission of the HRSC was to clean up the Hudson River, advocate its protection, and educate the public, including children about the river's beauty.

A young Pete and Toshi Seeger make music, with the Hudson River in the background.

The sloop was built to sail up and down the Hudson River to help the Clearwater organization promote its causes. The Seegers built a home in the Highlands overlooking the Hudson River. They both worked relentlessly and were successful in cleaning up the Hudson and making generations realize its beauty.

The Sloop Clearwater sails up the Hudson, in a photo by Anthony Pepitone.

courtesy Wiki Commons

One method of promoting the environmental and education mission was to have festivals along the Hudson every year. The Clearwater Festival, the Pumpkin Festival, the Corn Festival, and the Strawberry Festival were all successful.

Pete was selected to sing with Bruce Springsteen at President Barack Obama's inauguration. On Pete Seeger's 90th birthday, a celebration held in New York at Madison Square Garden and broadcast on PBS showed the respect his peers had for him. The following artists were there to sing his songs and honor him: Bruce Springsteen, Dave Matthews, Joan Baez, John Mellencamp, Richie Havens, Tom Paxton, Arlo Guthrie and others.

On July 9, 2013, Toshi died and Pete died not long afterward on Jan. 27, 2014. This picture is from the Beacon Pumpkin Festival on Oct. 13, 2013, the last festival on the Hudson that Pete attended. For the first time he was not there with his wife. After the festival ended and when everyone was packing up, Pete walked around by himself and looked around at the Hudson River that he helped clean up.

In 2013, Pete Seeger attended his last Pumpkin Festival in Beacon, New York. Photo by Christopher Cring

When Pete died there was an overwhelming, quick response. President Obama noted that Seeger had been called "America's tuning fork" *and that he believed in* "the power of song" *to bring social change.* "Over the years, Pete used his voice and his hammer to strike blows for workers' rights and civil rights, world peace, and environmental conservation. Pete always invited us to sing along, reminded us where we came from, and showed us where we needed to go. We will always be grateful to Pete Seeger."

Bruce Springsteen said of Seeger's death: "I lost a great friend and a great hero last night."

Summer 1975: Billy Joel moved to Highland Falls after spending three years in Los Angeles. Highland Falls is a small town on the Hudson just over the Bear Mountain Bridge across from Anthony's Nose. Billy Joel took a Greyhound bus and while on it wrote "New York State of Mind."

A Greyhound bus is juxtaposed with the road to Highland Falls.

While in Highland Falls, Billy Joel wrote the Turnstiles album, whose second song is "Summer, Highland Falls."

One of the most popular musical artists of all time, Billy Joel sells out major stadiums whenever he is on tour.

When Billy Joel was doing his Intrepid tour he spent time in the Hudson Valley and was inspired by the beauty. After leaving Los Angeles he rented a Highland Falls house that overlooked the Hudson River, with Anthony's Nose visible in the distance.

Now the house called Overlook, is a bed-and-breakfast.

Billy Joel rented this house in Highland Falls.

Sep. 11, 2001: Terrorists hijacked American Airlines flight 11 out of Logan Airport in Boston. With 81 passengers and 11 crew members aboard, the hijackers took over the plane and flew it to Albany and then down the Hudson River at low altitude, past Anthony's Nose. Continuing on, the plane eventually crashed into the World Trade Center, whose Twin Towers the terrorists targeted, at 8:46 a.m.

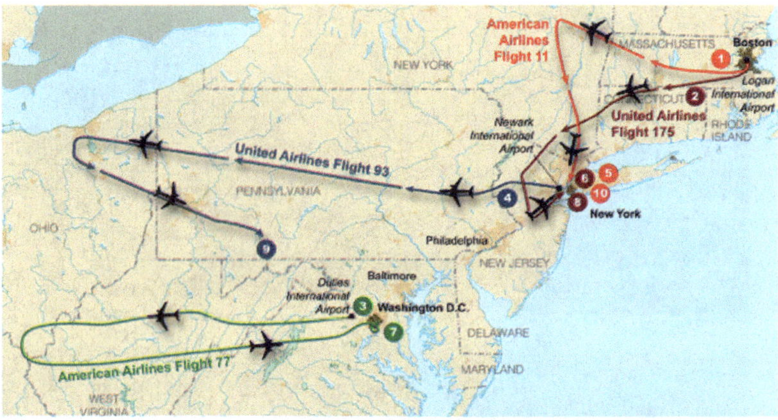

Paths of 9/11 flights: Flight labeled **1** *was out of Logan Airport in Boston. courtesy Wiki Commons*

A simulation depicts the view from the top of Anthony's Nose Mountain as the American Airlines plane flew by on that Tuesday morning, 9/11. The flight came at low altitude along the Hudson River, as reported by calls from passengers on the plane.

It was the first plane to strike the World Trade Center.

The 9/11 terrorists hijacked four planes. Two crashed into the World Trade Center in New York City, one crashed into the Pentagon, and the fourth crashed into a field in Pennsylvania when passengers revolted and prevented the plane from crashing into its designated target of a federal government building.

More than 3,000 people died from these attacks, the deadliest terrorist incident in the United States. Osama bin Laden of al-Qaeda claimed responsibility and was killed on May 2, 2011.

Photos taken after the World Trade Center attack include one (left) from The Federal Emergency Management Agency showing destruction and rescuers searching through the rubble and one (right) by Don Halasy of victims covered in dust helping each other. courtesy Wiki Commons

A few days later President George Bush went on the 9/11 rescue pile and gave his "bullhorn" speech next to firefighter Bob Beckwith to comfort and rally the United States and the world. He said:

"I want you all to know that America today, America today is on bended knee, in prayer for the people whose lives were lost here, for the workers who work here, for the families who mourn. This nation stands with the good people of New York City and New Jersey and Connecticut as we mourn the loss of thousands of our citizens."

In New York City, the 911 memorial at the site of the old World Trade Center quietly glows in a beautiful Photo by Dave Z., courtesy Wiki Commons

Sources for references throughout this book include Wikipedia, Wiki Commons, Founders.archive.gov and the Library of Congress.

Cover Design: Jason Cring

Cover photo: Christopher Cring, christopher.cring@gmail.com

Editor: Liz Schevtchuk Armsrtong

Made in the USA
Columbia, SC
13 April 2025

56440528R10070